AMMA'S CUISINE

Traditional to Fusion Sri Lankan &
International Recipes & an Island Wedding Story

Recipes and Stories by

LILANIE KADIRGAMAR GEIGER

Food Photography by

LUXSHMANAN NADARAJA

ISBN: 978-1-957203-38-6 (sc)
ISBN: 978-1-957203-39-3 (hc)
ISBN: 978-1-957203-40-9 (e)

The Ewings Publishing LLC
One Galleria Blvd., Suite 1900, Metairie, LA 70001
1-888-421-2397

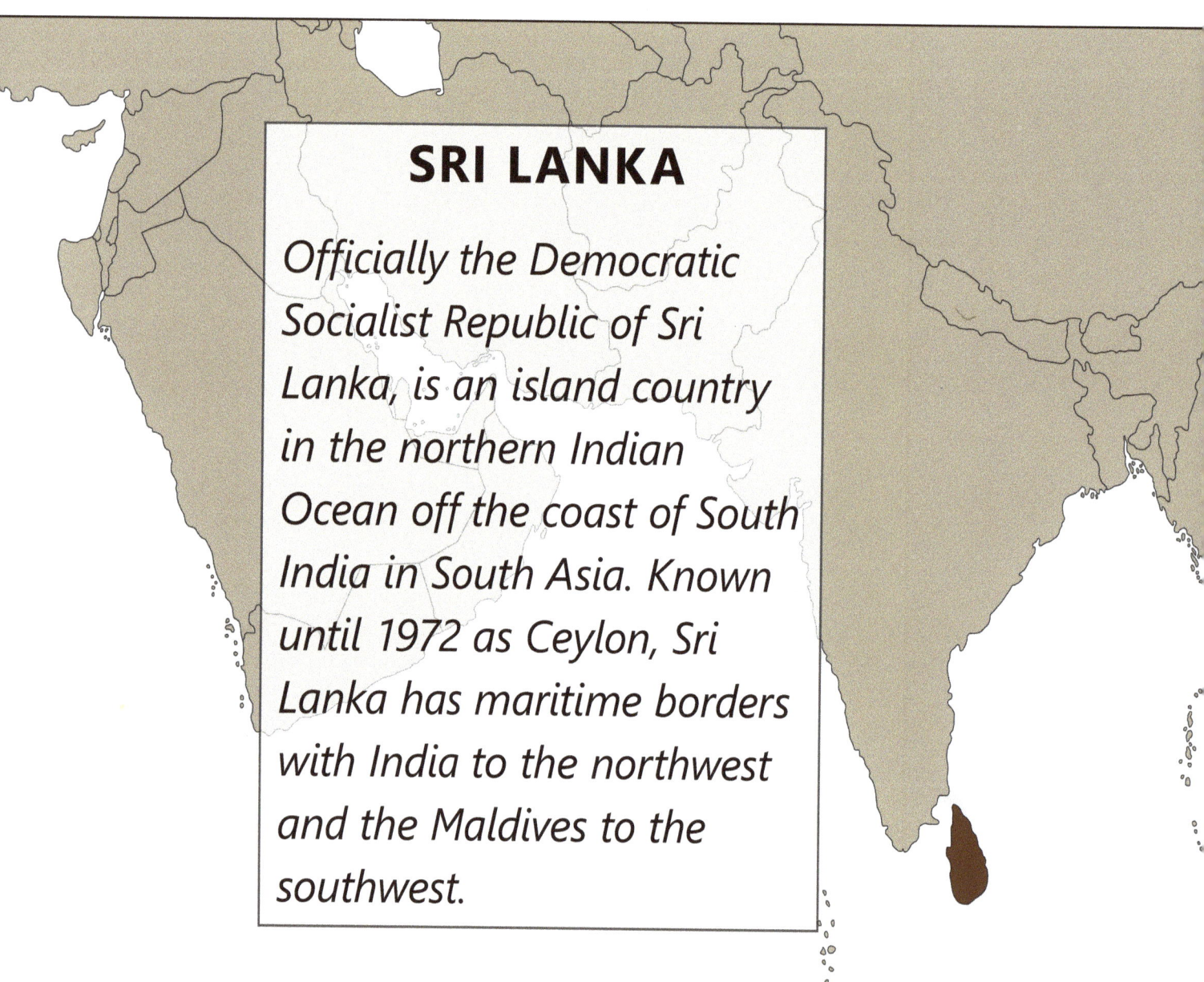

SRI LANKA

Officially the Democratic Socialist Republic of Sri Lanka, is an island country in the northern Indian Ocean off the coast of South India in South Asia. Known until 1972 as Ceylon, Sri Lanka has maritime borders with India to the northwest and the Maldives to the southwest.

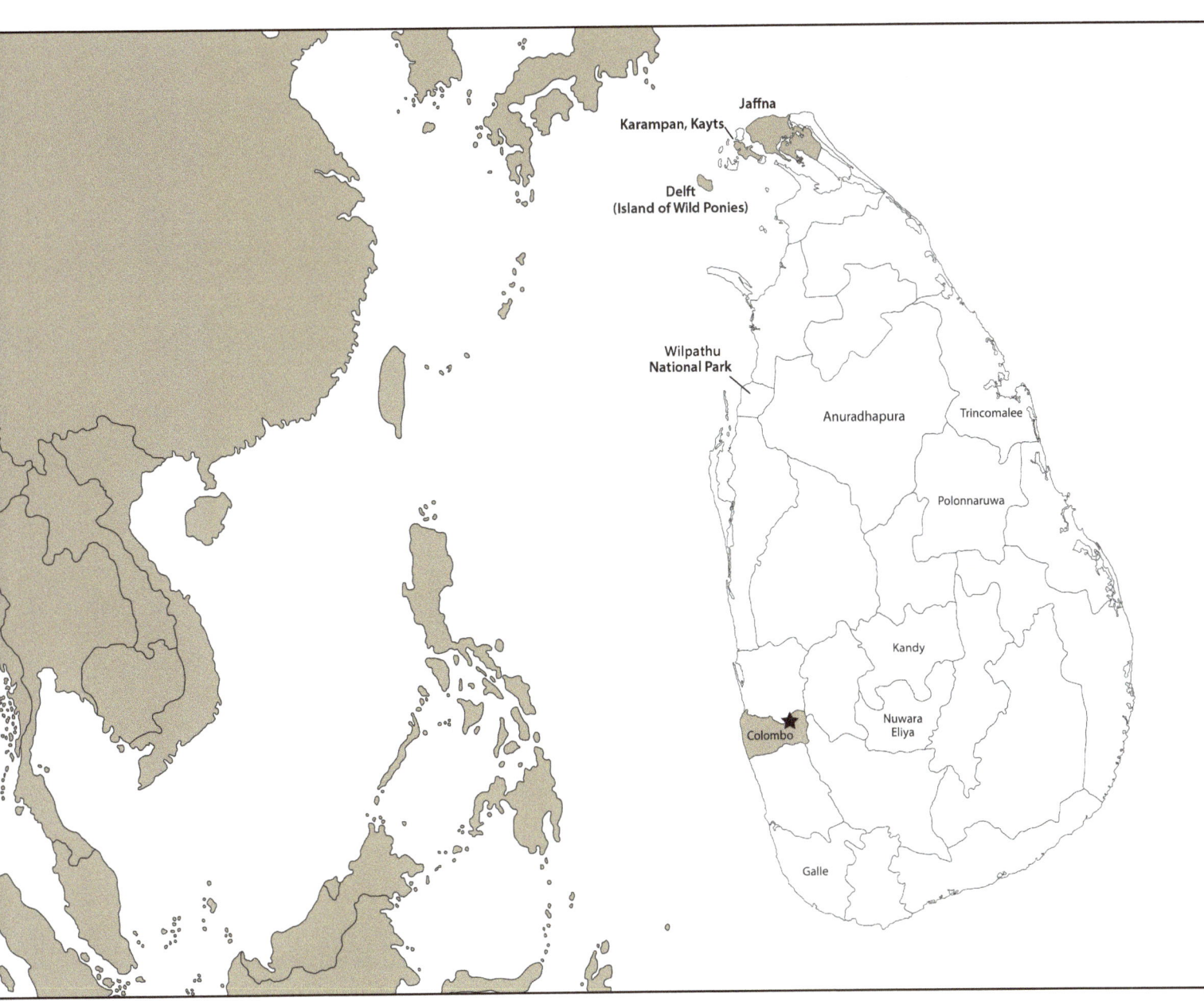

Jaffna

Karampan, Kayts

Delft
(Island of Wild Ponies)

Wilpathu
National Park

Anuradhapura

Trincomalee

Polonnaruwa

Kandy

Nuwara
Eliya

Colombo

Galle

My mother's sister Sukaniya listening to the musicians playing at dawn.

Dedication

This Cookbook is a Special Dedication to my mother Vasanthica, who has provided me with the greatest Inspiration – to honor and treasure her memory with this cook book. Her loving, generous and tireless energy, coupled with her intelligence and unmatched capabilities in the kitchen, makes me proud and privileged to share her unique talent with all: whether side-by-side, across the country, or around the world. A mother who gave her all, without question, to family, friends, and strangers alike.

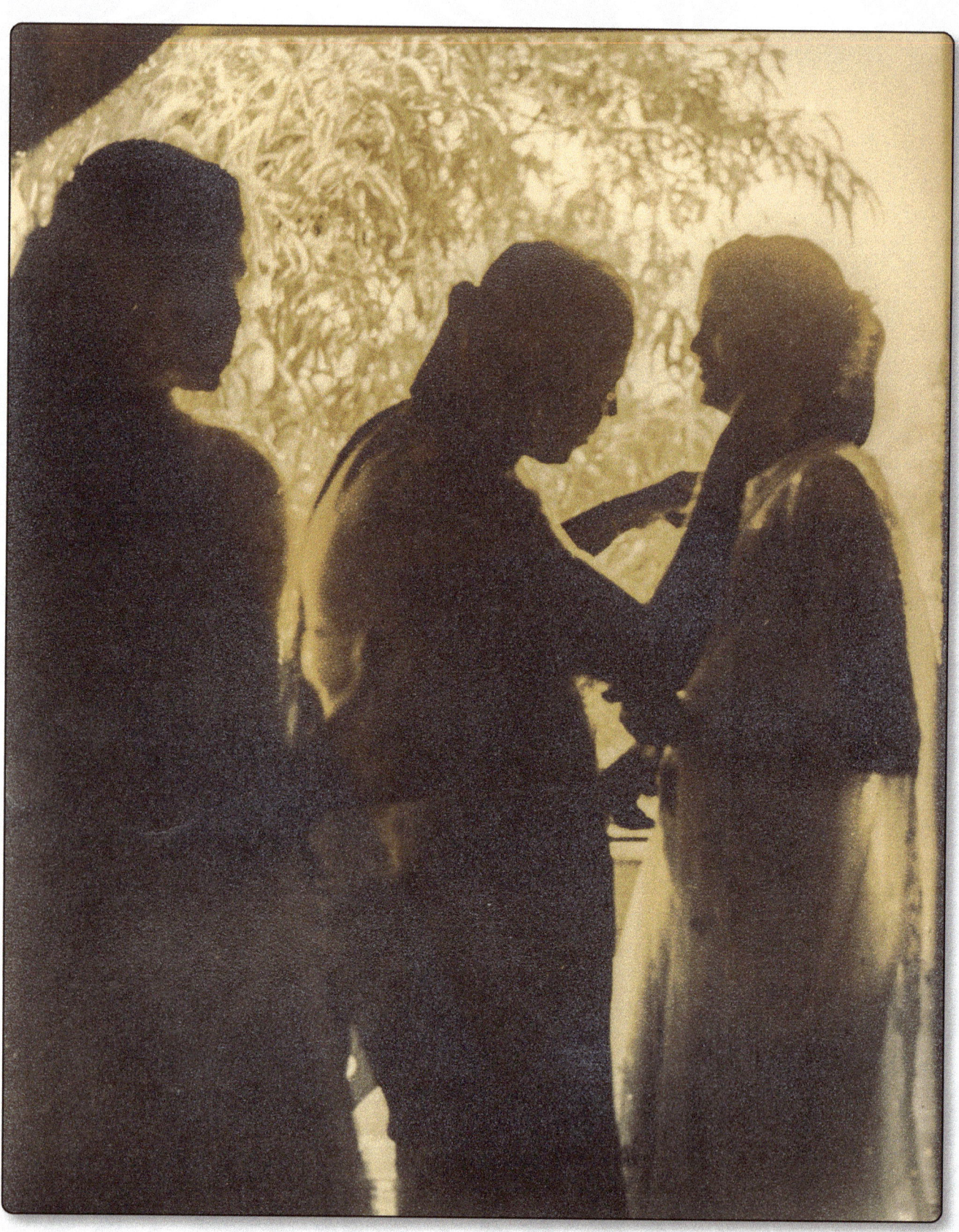

Bride being dressed by her adored Aunt Rajeswari.

Acknowledgements

This cookbook has been a project of mine that has been 12 years in the making. But as the saying goes "all good things take time". It all started with my dear friend Jose Andrade. I articulated to him my passion for cooking that I acquired from my Mother, and the idea of transferring my parents "Island Wedding" into a theme for my cookbook. Jose began my project with some cookbook software package he installed on my computer. Next we took some archaic digital camera shots of my dishes in our attempt to create this Island Wedding Story - Cookbook. He painstakingly helped me with several annoying tasks such as the glossary, temperature conversion, pagination and the like. The final draft was edited by him, and I am forever indebted to him for making my dream come true. Thank you, Jose for all your help and support.

I showed my initial draft to my first cousin Radhika Philip. She loved the concept and advised me to take this book to another level by having it done by professionals. This advice resulted in hiring a graphics designer, professional photographers and printers. Thank you Radhi for the best advice a cousin and friend could give.

Writing does not come easy for me as I am more mathematically inclined. So I simply wrote all my thoughts down for the introduction and description of the Island Wedding Story. I then shared it with my dearest aunt and close friend June Somasunderam Chanmugam. She edited my story and added the much needed historical dates on Sri Lanka, formerly known as Ceylon. She was also a close friend of my mother's, and her additional insight was invaluable. Thank you Aunty June.

My sister Ramani, the person I could always turn to in good times and bad. We are forever grateful for the love and inspiration taught to us by our parents. She established our family mantra – "Love Conquers All", which is what we attempt to live by daily. I thank you for adding your insight of our mother, and your exceptional writing skills that turned the written portions of this cookbook into a work of Art.

Thank you, Luxshman Nadaraja for the amazing photography that turned this cook book into an exotic depiction of culinary art. Additionally, his wife Nelun Harasgama who's artistic capabilities produced an amazing presentation for the food layout and design.

Jim Darling, my Graphic Designer who assumed he could take his time with completing the design because I took five years to complete the recipes, did an exceptional job. Thank you so much Jim, I could not have done it without you.

Thank you, Rebekah Pizana for your review and insightful and creative input.

Lastly, I would like to thank my dearest friend David Greenhill. With his faith and confidence in my cooking abilities, he embarked on the task of publishing my cookbook. He enabled me to be a visionary, and taught me how to reach for the stars. I thank you David, from the bottom of my heart.

The groom's sister Iswari arrives with her son,
Dayalan the page boy, to deliver the "Koorai" sari on a silver tray.

Introduction

Our story begins in Sri Lanka (formally known as Ceylon). It is an island nation in the form of a tear drop that lies just beneath the southern tip of India. It has often been called the pearl of the Indian Ocean. There begins our roots as the Tamil speaking community of Sri Lanka, who are predominantly located in the North of the country. The island, small as it may be, acquired an importance far in excess of its size as it lay on the trade route between Europe and Asia. It has been and continues to be valued, not only for its position but also for its Spice Gardens, its tropical beauty, and, above all, for its 'serendipity', a word coined from one of its old names, Serendib. In addition to playing host to early Arab traders from the 8th Century, it was invaded by the Cholas from South India, and in more recent times has been colonized, from the 16th Century on, by the Portuguese, the Dutch and the British, finally gaining Independence, in 1948 at the conclusion of WWII.

The influence of visitors and colonizer alike is to be found in the physical characteristics of its people. This is further exhibited in the country's languages, dress, religions, cultures and, last but not least, the influence on food. On the whole we are a somewhat polyglot lot, due to the influence of former colonizers. You will find evidence of this influence on food in this 'cookbook' which you may possibly recognize, and which I will acknowledge throughout the book.

Following in a long tradition of mothers everywhere, and to us as children, a tradition we saw as being particularly strong in our family, as my grandmother and my mother like her, loved to cook. It was one of the ways in which they demonstrated their undeniable love for us. While they cooked for the sheer pleasure that cooking gave them, above all else they cooked for the love of their family. Our earliest and most enduring memories center on food. Our grandmother, not to be outdistanced, would see to it that she had us at her house for lunch every day. To my mother fell the privilege of providing the remainder of our meals, which, though she might not have prepared them herself, was carefully supervised by her. But there were many instances such as birthdays and other special occasions when my mother prepared all the food herself with the help of her sous chefs, of course. She catered events for family and friends, and was known for her culinary abilities by all who knew her.

As immigrants to the United States in 1970, we came as a family which included my mother, father, sister and me. My mother qualified herself in Sri Lanka as a seamstress for infants and children's clothing – a skill the United States Government recognized as a

"Specialized Skill" and granted us Permanent Residency. This enabled us to arrive in the USA as "Permanent Residents", with the infamous green card in hand.

Having been denied the opportunity for a college education by her father, who instead schooled her in cooking and sewing classes, at the age of 45 she graduated "Cum Laude" from Boston University with a degree in accounting. She accomplished this feat while ensuring her husband and children acclimatized to a new country and a lifestyle that was foreign to them. She took all this in her stride and tackled all her challenges head-on. It has often been said of her – that she was in many ways simply ahead of her time. She was a remarkable woman and a great role model to her children.

Our mother developed into a unique and talented cook as she embraced the flavors of the Western World with the flavors of the Eastern World. She was innovative, imaginative, creative, and never tiring! We had taken much of all this for granted as children. Now older and wiser, we are able to recognize and acknowledge her for what she was, a truly generous and loving person. No effort was too much for her if it meant helping not just her family, but also her wider circle of friends, and strangers alike. She was known to mail parcels of food to young students, to cook and carry suitcases of food and cakes on planes when visiting family and friends. She seldom let anyone leave her home unless they had something exotic to eat or drink. Visitors always left with a generous parcel of food in hand. She had a heart of gold, and even in her latter years, stricken with ill health due to

diabetes, her endurance in the kitchen never failed.

I learnt a lot from my mother, not just about cooking, but about life and living. She taught me how to make the best with what you have and that giving is just as much fun as receiving. I remember vividly the love and care she gave me when my son was born, sparing no effort to see that I had my most favorite foods, elegantly served on a tray in my room. Now, I want to do the same for my son and for his wife when the time comes. And so the tradition continues...and my mother's spirit will always be with us.

A special trait of my mother's was her ability and willingness to share all her recipes – especially those that she had concocted herself. I know in my heart that she is thrilled beyond all joys that I am now making her recipes available to a much larger audience. Some of the recipes included in this cookbook come from her friends, as exchanging recipes played an important part in her life. As such, other recipes that you will find included in this cookbook have come to me from my sister Ramani and my friends.

"Amma's Cuisine" is compiled in loving memory of my mother. It is named as such, as Amma is the Tamil name for mother.

East meets west in both traditional and colonial attire, as they await the arrival of the wedding party under the shade of the trees.

Bride leaving for the church on the arm of her father Pedropillai.

An Island Wedding

I want this tribute to my mother to be more than just a cookbook that may be placed on a shelf amongst other cookbooks. I want to tell you a story – a story of an"Island Wedding". The pictures presented in this cookbook are of my parents' wedding day. It will illustrate a story of their wedding on the island of Kayts, off the Jaffna Peninsula in Sri Lanka. The wedding ceremony was held in the town church, a catholic church that is located next door to my great grandmother's house. The wedding reception thereafter was held at my grandfather's house named: "Sudha Sagaram", in the town of Karampan.

As you follow through the pictures in this cookbook you will notice the western traditions intermingled with eastern dress and traditions. Our families are descendants of Christian converts with Hindu roots. My mother's family is Roman Catholic and my father's family is Methodist. My father, however, was the only sibling from his family that converted to Catholicism as a young man. We are spiritually Christian with Tamil traditions that are linked to our ancestral Hindu roots.

My sister and I spent all our holidays with our grandparents on this island, and now 39 years later still hold onto the vivid memories of days gone by. A few years ago I took my first cousins and my son back to the war ravaged town of Karampan, Kayts, and told them all the stories of our family gatherings. Stories of when we rode in our great grandmother's Bullock cart, bathed from water in the well, and ran across the paddy fields to our Great-grandmother's house. Remembrance of how I played house with colorful little clay pots using leaves to make a curry, caterpillars that stung upon touch, and the skinny toddy tapper who came at dawn to climb up the palm tree and tap fresh toddy to drink. My grandmother insisted on the "Catch of the day" as our fish was picked up as soon as the fisherman landed on shore. We would have fresh Shrimp in "Raal Sothi" (see page 52) with a rice flour dish called Puttu.

I dedicate this passage to my Philip cousins, all the female descendants of the Thambiayah Clan (pretty much the whole town), Pedropillai and Gertrude Philip, their children Vasanthica, Rajan (known as Bole Philip), Sukaniya, my wonderful father Selvanathan Kadirgamar (affectionately referred to as "Bhai"), my sister Ramani and lastly to my son Michael Selvanathan who found his future by journeying into the past.

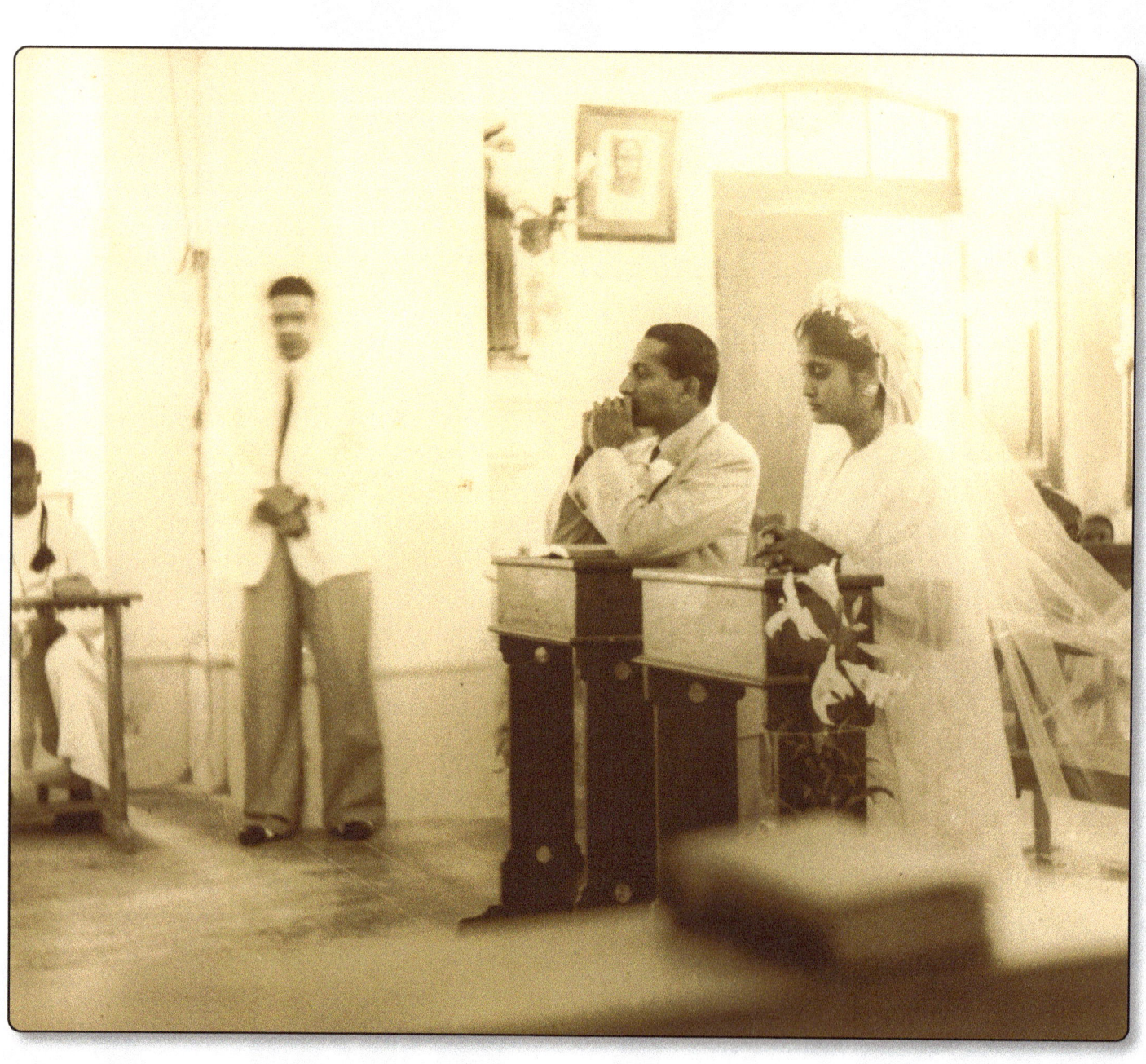

Bride and groom leaving the church, whose land was donated by our great grandfather, as the nuns and priests had to travel far to get to this parish

THE RECIPES

(Clockwise from Left): Chili Eggs, Indonesian Fried Rice, and Indonesian Pork Satay.

APPETIZERS & SOUP

A "teaser" to whet your appetite
as we begin our journey.

Several people have asked me how my parents met. In fact it was an arranged marriage which meant that Amma would bring a dowry (cash and/or property) with her into the marriage. Amma, (name for mother in Tamil), was given three pictures of eligible men and from those she chose my father. A meeting was then arranged and they were permitted to go out together provided they were chaperoned on their dates, both before and after, their formal engagement.

CRAB MUFFINS

Every time I visit Sri Lanka someone would reminisce about these crab muffins. This delectable recipe was created by my mother and ultimately became her signature breakfast dish. Her houseguests would wake up to the delicious smells of her cooking. The crab muffins would be baking in the oven while she was whipping up a cherry cake for her friend Mrs. Fredrickson. The family is fairly certain that she added the green chilies to a basic recipe she picked up from a magazine to spice it up.

1 lb	cooked crabmeat
12	English muffins
2 jars	(5 oz jar) Old English cheese spread
½ (2 oz)	stick butter, softened
1	green chili, chopped

SERVING SIZE: 24 PREPARATION TIME: 30 MINS

Mix butter and cheese spread until soft. Add crab and chopped green chili.

Slice muffins in two. Spread crab mixture on each half and bake at 350°F for 15 minutes.

Slice into halves or quarters to serve as appetizer, or leave as is, to serve as a breakfast dish.

Note: Slices of bread can be substituted for English muffins. Velveeta cheese or Kraft soft cheese in cans or packets can be substituted for the Old English cheese spread.

HUMMUS

This recipe heralds from the kitchen of my dear neighbor and friend, Arjunia Oakley. It is by far one of the best hummus dishes I have ever had. She received private cooking lessons from my mother for some of her signature dishes. Arjunia and George Oakley were the first neighbor's to greet us when we moved into our home on Aurora Dr, Kensington, Maryland. They have been a great support system to me and my family and I treasure their friendship. Arjunia is of Palestinian decent and we have similar interest in cooking and she has introduced me to the wonderful flavors of Palestinian food. My favorite is her meat pies. She also makes her traditional bread which looks like pita and tastes great, especially hot out of the oven with some butter. I always make sure I visit her when she is baking bread.

Hummus reminds me of a work trip to Cyprus and having mezza with hummus at an outdoor restaurant along with their local brew and the evening ending with us dancing on the tables. On another trip to Cyprus we passed a "Gentleman's Club" and I asked the local colleague what it was and he just laughed. After dinner they took me there and played the biggest joke on me by having a Russian woman do a table dance just for me.

1 can	chick peas (15 oz can)
½	lemon, squeezed
⅛ cup	tahini, or peanut butter with a dash of sesame oil
1 clove	garlic (large clove) smashed and cut up
	dash cayenne pepper
	salt
	paprika
⅛ cup	pine nuts, sautéed in olive oil
	olive oil
3 loaves	pita bread, heated in the oven

SERVING SIZE: 20
PREPARATION TIME: 20 MINUTES

Drain peas and reserve liquid.

Combine the chick peas, garlic, tahini, cayenne pepper, salt to taste, lemon juice and half the reserved liquid. Put it into a food processor and blend. Add more of the reserved liquid, and salt if required.

To assemble, spread mixture on a platter in the center, sprinkle with olive oil and paprika on top. Top with pine nuts.

Cut up pita into serving pieces and arrange around a platter.

STUFFED MUSHROOMS

Growing up in Sri Lanka mushrooms was unknown to me as they were not a local product. Mushrooms are used in a variety of ways that are quite interesting. For example, the hippie era in the 70's used a variety of mushroom as a hallucinogen. My friend Siva eats a variety in a tablet form called "Ganoderma" from a particular place in East Malaysia that cleanses the blood. The most popular is the consumption of my completely vegetarian."

Stuffed Mushrooms" that are best served as an appetizer.

1 lb	**mushrooms**
2 tblsps	**oil**
1 clove	**garlic, crushed**
½	**onion, chopped**
⅓	**cup bread crumbs**
1 tblsp	**parsley, chopped**
⅛ tsp	**oregano**
3 tblsps	**Parmesan cheese, grated**
½ tsp	**salt**

SERVING SIZE: 10
PREPARATION TIME: 40 MINS

Preheat oven to 400°F.

Wash and dry mushrooms. Remove stems and place mushroom caps on a baking tray.

Chop stems. Heat oil in a frying pan over medium heat.

Add garlic and onions and sauté for a few seconds.

Add stems and sauté for 10 minutes.

Mix bread crumbs, parsley, oregano, cheese and salt together.

Add to mixture in the frying pan and stir for 3 minutes.

Turn off fire.

Fill mushroom caps with mixture and bake for 20 minutes.

PUMPKIN SOUP

This is a tasty Australian soup that can be easily adapted for various types of pumpkin and squash. Recipe given to me by Sally Burford, we became friends in Kuantan, Malaysia, when I worked there in 1995 for a couple of years. My son and I traveled to Australia the summer before we left Malaysia. Our first stop was Sydney; he loved to skateboard down all the steps in Sydney Harbor. We then went by train to Melbourne, but stopped on the way to visit Sally. The country side was beautiful and while we were at a park a flock of white and pink cockatoos flew by and stopped right near us. It was amazing, especially considering my love of birds.

2 lbs	**Asian pumpkin, peeled and cut into large pieces**
1 med	**onion, sliced**
2 tblsps	**butter**
1 tblsp	**corn flour (starch)**
4 cups	**boiling water**
1 large	**cube (or two small cubes) of chicken bouillon**
⅛ tsp	**ground nutmeg or cloves–optional**
½ cup	**milk or cream**

SERVING SIZE: 8 PREPARATION TIME: 1 HR 20 MINS

Dissolve chicken bouillon in boiling water.

Sauté pumpkin and onion in butter for about 10 minutes. Add corn flour/starch. When heated through, cover with chicken stock. You may add cloves or nutmeg.

Simmer covered until cooked and mushy about ½ to 1 hour. Put soup in blender or food processor and blend. Return soup to pot and add milk or cream and reheat until hot.

Note: Buy the brightest pumpkin. Asian pumpkins can be bought at any Asian food market. To make this soup vegetarian add vegetable bouillon instead of chicken bouillon.

STUFFED CAPSICUM (SWEET BANANA PEPPERS)

Nothing beats stuffing a sweet banana pepper with a jazzed up tuna concoction. A popular short eat in Sri Lanka and the recipe was given to me by my mother which is as unique as she was. It can be made with hot peppers as well. A similar dish is also made in Sri Lanka into a curry by stuffing whole peppers with the same aromatic tuna fish mixture, battering it, frying it, and then adding it to a curry sauce.

1 can	tuna in water–drained (6oz or 170g)
½ med	onion, chopped fine
4 tblsps	butter (for albacore; 2 tblsps for chunk light)
1 tblsp	ketchup or chili sauce (or half of each)
1 tblsp	parsley–chopped
4	sweet bananas peppers or hot capsicums, washed and dried
8	pats butter

SERVING SIZE: 8 PREPARATION TIME: 30 MINUTES

Preheat oven to 350°F.

Sauté onions in 4 tblsps butter until soft. Add ketchup/chili sauce and parsley. Let it cook a minute longer and add the fish. Mix and cook for 3 minutes.

Split the peppers lengthwise and remove seeds. Stuff the peppers with the tuna mixture and top with a pat of butter.

Bake for 20 minutes. Arrange on a platter and serve.

Note: Boiled fish can be substituted for a can of tuna. Use a thick fish.

INDONESIAN PORK SATAY

I purchased a grill thirty years ago and obtained the recipe with my new grill and much like my mother I have changed it to suit my tastes. Inspired by my son's love for sate, this recipe has evolved to be a family favorite. When we lived in Malaysia, we would buy assorted sate (no pork) from "Sate Zul" at least once a week. It was a small sate shop in Kuantan that cooked the sate using coconut shells for charcoal and they would cook them outside on specific sate grills that were wide and long enough to balance the sate on the grill. There are two different spellings for the word, "sate" and "satay". The word "sate" originated in 1595 and stems from the word to satiate, which means to satisfy fully. Sate is a popular appetizer in Thai, Indonesian and Malaysian food.

3 lbs	boneless, lean pork
¼ cup	peanut oil
¼ cup	soy sauce
1 tblsp	chopped onion
1 clove	garlic, crushed
1 tsp	sugar
⅛ tsp	curry powder
30 6-inch	bamboo skewers
PEANUT SAUCE	
1 ½ tblsp	coconut powder
¾ cup	milk, heated
2 tblsps	butter
½ tsp	curry powder
1 med	onion, finely chopped
½ tsp	ginger root, minced
1 clove	garlic, minced
½ cup	crushed pineapple
3 tblsps	peanut butter
2 tblsps	sugar
½ tsp	salt
½ cup	chicken stock
	freshly ground pepper

SERVING SIZE: 15 PREPARATION TIME: 1 HR 45 MIN

Cut the pork into 1 ¼ inch strips. Combine the peanut oil with the soy sauce, onion, garlic, sugar, and curry powder.

Stir in the pork and refrigerate from 2 hours to overnight. (Recommend overnight).

Soak skewers in boiling water for one hour. Thread the pork strips onto the skewers.

In the meantime, to make the PEANUT SAUCE, add the coconut powder to the hot milk. Heat the butter in a skillet. Add the curry powder and cook, stirring for 1 to 2 minutes. Add the onion, ginger root and garlic and sauté, stirring for 5 minutes. Add the coconut milk and remaining ingredients. Stir to blend. Cook covered, on a low fire, stirring occasionally, for 20 minutes. Serve warm.

Grill the pork skewers outdoors on a grill. Keep turning them frequently so they do not burn.

Note: Use good quality pork such as boneless tenderloin. If you have to cook the pork indoors, broil for 6 to 10 minutes turning the pork frequently.

Parents of the bride, Archie and Pata (my grandparents)
awaiting the arrival of the bridal couple at home for the reception.

WONTONS

I credit this recipe to an old colleague Marc, who learned this dish during his tour in the Armed Forces while stationed in Hawaii. Marc and I worked together at a company called Satellite Business Systems and I am very glad to have made his acquaintance. So much so that he and his wife were in attendance at my wedding and he had such a funny sense of humor and was quite taken with all the women in saris. He called it a "sari" (sorry) occasion. A sari is the traditional dress worn by Sri Lankan and Indian women. My mother was most comfortable in a sari. Hence after she graduated from college as an accountant in the USA, she was unable to get a job in Corporate America as she wore a sari to work every day and, at that time, in the 70's, it was an unacceptable mode of dress. I wore sari to work once a year in the summer and all my coworkers were so respectful to me, almost held me in reverence.

½ lb	**minced pork**
6 med	**shrimp, chopped**
¼ cup	**scallion, minced (spring onions)**
½	**sm can water chestnuts, drained**
1 tblsp	**ginger, minced**
2 tsps	**soy sauce**
⅛ tsp	**pepper**
1 pkg	**wonton skins**
1 cup	**peanut oil for deep fat frying**
1 bottle	**duck sauce**

SERVING SIZE: 15 PREPARATION TIME: 1 HR 30 MINS

Place the first 7 ingredients on a chopping board.

Chop everything together, mixing well while chopping.

Place half a tsp of mixture on the center of each wonton skin. Fold in half like an envelope.

Use water or egg yolk to glue the sides together. Take the two long corners and glue together with water or egg yolk.

Heat oil at a medium high temperature in a wok or deep fryer.
Fry wontons in the hot peanut oil until golden.

Drain on paper towels and serve with duck sauce.

MULLIGATAWNY

Mulligatawny means pepper water in my native tongue: Tamil. This recipe was given to me by my mother. She had this knack of taking traditional recipes and improving them. If you Google mulligatawny you will find hundreds and hundreds of recipes for this soup. The variations to the basic recipe are very interesting. It is great to drink when one is not feeling well.

1 lb	chicken bones
1 med	onion, sliced or quartered
3 med	carrots sliced big
4 cups	water
2 cloves	garlic
1 large	tomato, quartered
1 med	onion sliced thin
1 cube	chicken bouillon
½ tsp	curry powder
½ tsp	black pepper
½ tsp	chili powder
1 small	onion chopped
1 tblsp	evaporated milk
1 tblsp	coconut powder
3 lbs	chicken wings skin removed

SERVING SIZE: 10 PREPARATION TIME: 1 HR 30 MINS

Make a stock by boiling chicken bones with water, carrots and onions.
Strain it for a long time using a cheesecloth.

Put the stock in a pan and boil again with garlic, tomatoes, onions and a bouillon cube.

Add curry powder, black pepper, and chili powder and continue to boil.

In a pan, fry the chopped onion until golden brown. Add to the stock, evaporated milk and coconut powder.

Add chicken wings and boil further until meat is cooked about 20 minutes. Take it off the fire. Remove the chicken from the soup, debone the meat and put the meat back into the soup, heat and serve.

Fried Chicken Dorothy and Corn Salad

MAIN DISHES

Amma's delectable curries from her hometown Karampan and dishes from various countries and cultures within the USA.

I believe my parents went into the jungles of Sri Lanka for their honeymoon. This at the time (early 1950's) was a very adventurous endeavor. They went into the Wilpattu National Park where they were chased by a wild elephant. Amma who had just got her driver's license was in the driver's seat while my dad scared off the elephant with a shot in the air.

BAKED CRAB

A scrumptious dish served in homes and restaurants in Sri Lanka and has several variations with the addition of ingredients like cheese, hot chili and condiments into the crab mixture and stuffed into real crab shells. My mother's version is simple and delicious.

Thinking of baked crab brings back memories of my teenage years, having dinner at nightclubs by the sea, the Little Hut in Mount Lavinia, La Langoustri by the beach, where they served dinner and we danced until the wee hours of the morning. They were such innocent times. To some of us who are now living in the West for more than twenty years relate to "Those were the days, my friend".

We had to wait for nearly a year to get our visa to the States and, during that time, our group of friends would go out every night and we would use the excuse that we were having farewell parties for me. My father was quite shocked at me and questioned why I had to go out almost every night. I asked him to please let me enjoy myself because my life was going to change drastically when we went to America. It sure did. I learned what it was like to work two part-time jobs and go to College at the same time. The social butterfly turned into an engineer and surprised her class mates at St. Bridget's convent.

1 lb	**cooked lump crabmeat**
2 ozs	**butter (½ stick)**
1 small	**onion, chopped, fine**
1	**egg**
1 sm can	**evaporated milk (5oz)**
½ can	**water (2.5oz)**
2 tblsps	**parsley, chopped**
1 tblsp	**ketchup**
	dash pepper
½ tsp	**salt**
8 small	**crab shells**

SERVING SIZE: 8 PREPARATION TIME: 45 MINUTES
Preheat oven to 350°F.

Beat the egg. Add milk, water, salt, pepper, ketchup, and chopped parsley to the beaten egg and mix. Sauté onions in butter on medium heat until soft, about 5 minutes. Add crab to the onions, mix, and sauté for a few seconds. Pour custard (egg and milk mixture) into pan and mix. Remove pan from fire.

Spoon the mixture into crab shells. Dust with breadcrumbs. Place shells on a baking tray. (Baking dish or Ramekin shells can be used)

Bake until set, about 20 minutes.

FRIED CHICKEN DOROTHY

Dorothy was a good friend of my mother's and they met at a catering place they both worked at. My mom worked as an accountant, not as a caterer. Dorothy and her husband were very helpful to her and she taught my mother how to make her special fried chicken. My mother with her friend Dorothy's help made this dish as an entrée at my sister's wedding for 250 guests. Unfortunately I lost touch with them when my mother retired to Sri Lanka and we moved to Malaysia.

8	chicken legs, skinless
2 cloves	garlic, chopped
1 tsp	fresh ginger, chopped fine
¼ cup	light soy sauce
1 tsp	chicken seasoning
1 large	egg
1 tblsp	water
½ tsp	chicken seasoning
1 cup	bread crumbs
1 cup	oil
2 tblsp	honey

SERVING SIZE: 8 PREPARATION TIME: 1 HR 30 MINS

Mix chicken legs with 1 tsp chicken seasoning, garlic, ginger, light soy sauce and marinade for at least 1 hour.

Beat the egg with 1 tablespoon of water. Add ½ tsp chicken seasoning to breadcrumbs.

Dip chicken legs in egg mixture, coat with breadcrumbs.

Deep fry in hot oil (add more oil if required). Drain on paper towels.

Pour honey on chicken and serve.

Note: The chicken seasoning is the US version from McCormick known as Fried Chicken seasoning. Any other fried chicken seasoning can be substituted.

HAM WITH SHERRY

Recipe I picked up from the Andalusia region of Spain. Growing up in Sri Lanka my Mom made ham from a leg of pork for Christmas. The grocery store did not sell ham, so it had to be home made. I loved Christmas in Sri Lanka when I was growing up. We would get a Coniferous tree from the highlands where the weather was cooler. Santa would bring our gifts in a pillow case. On Christmas Eve while my mother took us shopping, Santa would drop off an envelope from the North Pole. My sister and I found the letters on the veranda when we came home and they were ice cold.

We would go to family parties on Christmas Eve and my father's side of the family always had a Nativity play. I remember being "Mary". My dad, who was the only Catholic in his family, would take us to midnight mass, and afterwards we had Christmas cake and honey wine. We ate special Western food for our Christmas dinners. For breakfast we had a special bread with golden raisins called Broeder (Dutch origin) which we ate with butter and Edam cheese. We still maintain these traditions with our own families in our home in the USA.

4 lbs	cooked ham
2 cups	sweet sherry, not cooking sherry
½ cup	raisins
1 cup	dried apricots, cut in half
1 cup	apricot nectar or water

SERVING SIZE: 15 PREPARATION TIME: 1 HR 30 MINS

Pre-heat the oven to 350° F

Score the ham in a diamond pattern. If there is skin on the ham trim the skin and leave some fat on it.

Place the meat in a roasting pan and pour the sherry over the meat. Cover with Aluminum foil.

Roast for 40 minutes in the preheated oven.

In the meantime, soak the raisins and apricots in the apricot nectar (recommend using apricot nectar instead of water). Remove the foil from the ham. Pour in the fruit and liquid onto the ham and cook for another 40 minutes basting the ham with the pan juices.

Slice the ham and arrange on a platter, pour the sauce over the ham and serve.

The couple are garlanded with fresh fragrant flowers by the bride's favorite Aunt and Uncle, Rajeswari and Alfred.

Marinated Pork Tenderloin with Cold Sesame Noodles

MARINATED PORK TENDERLOIN

Pork, I found out, was not a popular meat in Ceylon before World War II and was considered an unclean meat, as the Buddhist and Hindus were vegetarian and the Muslims do not eat pork. The British troops who came there during the war ate lots of pork and so did the "Burgher" community. Now, it is a very popular dish, especially "Black Pork Curry" made famous by the Burghers.

Burghers are a Eurasian ethnic group in Sri Lanka, consisting for the most part of male-line descendants of European colonists from the 16th to 20th centuries (mostly Portuguese, Dutch, German, and British) and local women, with some minorities of Swedish, Norwegian, French, and Irish.

I, of course, love both the black pork curry as well as wild boar curry which we get in the countryside and jungles of Sri Lanka. This dish is an Asian fusion meat that can be served with eastern or western sides.

2	pork tenderloins
¼ cup	soy sauce
3 tblsps	sugar
2 tblsps	onion, minced
2 tsps	ground ginger
2 cloves	garlic, minced
¼ cup	sesame seeds
1 tblsp	oil

SERVING SIZE: 6 PREPARATION TIME: 1 HR

Trim the fat from the tenderloins.

Combine the remaining ingredients except the oil in a bowl. Marinate the pork in the mixture three hours in the refrigerator or overnight, turning and basting frequently. Drain and reserve the marinade.

Preheat oven to moderate (375°F).

Transfer the pork to an oiled (using 1 tblsp oil) roasting pan and roast until tender, about 45 minutes.

Simmer the marinade for ten minutes.

Cut the pork into thin slices and place them on a platter and pour heated marinade on top and serve.

Note: This dish is usually served with fried rice and a green vegetable like Chinese broccoli (pronounced Kai Lan in Malaysia) sautéed in oil with fresh garlic or with scalloped potatoes and asparagus.

ROAST LEG OF LAMB

This succulent dish is attributed to my mother. She was given a 1972 edition of the Fanny Farmer Cookbook from our sponsor to America Mrs. Edith Weyerhaeuser, one of the kindest and most caring persons I have ever met. I have the original tattered copy and my sister has a newer version since it is a family tradition in our house to use this cookbook as a great reference for original, tasty American food.

3 ½ lbs	leg of lamb
3 cloves	garlic, sliced ⅛ inch thick
1 tblsp	apricot jam or jelly
1 tblsp	mint sauce
1 tblsp	flour
1 cup	boiling water
1 cube	chicken bouillon, optional
	salt and pepper to taste
GRAVY	
1 tblsp	flour
1 cup	boiling water
½	chicken bouillon, optional

SERVING SIZE: 8 PREPARATION TIME: 2 HRS

Preheat oven to 325°F.

Make 10 shallow slits in the lamb with a sharp knife and tuck a thin sliver of garlic in each.

Roast lamb for 1 ½ hours.

Mix the apricot jam with the mint sauce. Glaze the lamb with the apricot and mint mixture and roast for another ½ hour.

Take the lamb out of the pan and place on a cutting board. Slice lamb and arrange on a platter.

GRAVY

To make the gravy, place the pan on the fire on low heat and throw out some of the fat or pour the pan drippings into a cup and let the fat rise to the top. Spoon out the fat and put the remaining drippings with a little fat back into the roasting pan.

Put a tblsp of flour in the pan and scrape the pan and let the flour cook for a few seconds. Add some salt and pepper and a cup of boiling water or a chicken bouillon dissolved in a cup of boiling water. Cook until the gravy thickens. Remove from the fire.

Pour over the sliced lamb or serve separately in a gravy boat.

COCONUT SHRIMP

I discovered recently that my son loved this dish which he ate at a bar in Seaside Heights where the television reality show "Jersey Shore" was filmed. It is also one of my favorite dishes. I make this dish with my mom's curry powder. The dish makes me think of Hawaii where I was fortunate enough to go on a business trip and it was just wonderful. Beautiful beaches, lovely vegetation and great snorkeling, I saw gorgeous colored fish and find I am always comparing the fish I see to those I saw in Malaysia in Tioman Island, while snorkeling off a boat with my son, where we saw very large Rainbow, Angel fish and many more varieties.

In Hawaii, a dish I thought was interesting, and which I liked, is the breakfast Sushi with fried spam sandwiched between the rice.

2 lbs	jumbo shrimp, shelled and deveined (30 raw)
¼ cup	lemon juice
½ tsp	salt
1 ½ tsps	curry powder
¼ tsp	ginger powder
2 cups	flour
1 ⅓ cups	milk
2 tsps	baking powder
7 oz	sweetened coconut flakes
1 cup	vegetable oil

SERVING SIZE: 10 PREPARATION TIME: 1 HR 30 MINS

Split the shrimp lengthwise with a sharp knife, but do not cut entirely through. Remove the vein.

Combine the lemon juice, salt, curry powder and ginger and marinate the shrimp in the mixture for one hour or longer. Recommend overnight.

Mix the flour, milk and baking powder thoroughly, remove shrimp from marinade. Add marinade to the batter and mix.

Dredge the shrimp with additional flour, dip in the batter and roll in coconut. Deep fry in hot oil until golden about 5 minutes.

Drain on paper towel and serve while hot.

SOUTHERN STEAK

Southern food is distinctly different and this recipe was given to me by my dear friend Sammy Gail Johnson. She taught me the basics of southern cooking, which I use to improve some of my recipes. I don't eat much steak anymore; however, I remember my college days at Northeastern, where my dorm mates and I went weekly to a steak house on Huntington Avenue in Boston where they served a T-bone steak, baked potato, a roll and a drink for $7.99. I love Southern cooking and have learned to make several dishes and recently learned to cook shrimp and grits and fried chicken with waffles.

1 lb	**cubed steak**
⅓ cup	**flour**
1 large	**onion cut into ¼ inch rings**
½	**stick or 2 oz butter**

SERVING SIZE: 4 PREPARATION TIME: 1 HR 30 MINS

Preheat oven to 350°F.

Place the flour in a plastic or paper bag, put steak in the bag and shake steak in flour.

Melt butter in frying pan on low fire, add onion rings and cook for two minutes.
Add steak and cook for about 30 minutes until steak is nicely brown. Make sure it is slow cooked.

Put contents of frying pan (steak & onion mixture) into a casserole dish with a cover.
Place in oven for about 30 minutes with a bit of water and cover the dish.

Take out of the oven and thoroughly enjoy it as my friend Sammy Gail would say and serve with a green vegetable such as collard greens.

Note: Cubed steak is a steak pounded with a mallet.

BEEF RENDANG

This is what the younger generation would call a banging dish! My favorite Beef Rendang was in Telok Chempadek at a Chinese restaurant by the beach in Kuantan. They served it garnished with pieces of fresh pineapple. It is very popular among my friends and it is also a part of the Indonesian "Rijstaeffel" (rice table).

My friend Jeff I., whom I fondly call the "Diva", has a running joke about Beef Rendang. He makes a face when he speaks the words and drags it out. Jeff surprised me, by making some great food when our friend Jeff W. and I visited him on Boxing Day in 2012, in Norway. I absolutely loved the salted lamb, a dish the Norwegians eat during the holidays and an unusual vegetable side dish of mashed rhubarb, squash and potato, and the wonderful breakfasts cooked by Alex.

It was an exceptional Christmas holiday as I spent it in Houston with my sister's family and my son and I flew back together on Christmas night to Newark, NJ and I continued on to Norway. On Christmas Eve and Christmas morning I sat outside in summer clothes and a day later I was in Oslo looking at the most beautiful white Christmas I had ever seen. I arrived the day after it had snowed heavily. We went up to the mountains and soaked in the outdoor hot tubs and enjoyed the beautiful mountains covered in snow.

Beef Rendang on the other hand reminds me of the beautiful beaches in the East coast of West Malaysia, facing the South China seas. Terengganu, Redang, Perhentian, Tioman. The West coast of course boasts of Penang and Langkawi.

3 lbs	round steak or roast		1 tsp	chili powder (optional for spicy)
2 medium	onions, roughly chopped		2 tsps	ground coriander
6 cloves	garlic		6	curry leaves
1 tblsp	fresh ginger, chopped		1 stem	fresh lemon grass or 3 strips lemon rind
3	fresh red chilies, seeded		1 tsp	Laos' powder
1 cup	canned coconut milk		½ cup	tamarind liquid, see Note 2 below
1 cup	prepared coconut milk, see Note 1 below		2 tsps	sugar
1 ½ tsps	salt		4	canned or fresh pineapple rings
1 tsp	ground turmeric			

SERVING SIZE: 12 PREPARATION TIME: 3 HOURS

Cut beef into strips about 1 inch wide and 1 inch long and ¼ inch thick.

Put onion, garlic, ginger, and chilies in blender container with half cup of canned coconut milk. Cover and blend until smooth. Pour into a large saucepan and wash out blender with remaining canned and prepared coconut milk. Add to saucepan all remaining ingredients except tamarind liquid and sugar. Mix well, add meat and bring quickly to the boil.

Reduce heat to moderate, add tamarind liquid and cook uncovered, until gravy is thick, stirring occasionally. Turn heat to medium low and continue cooking until gravy is almost dry, stirring frequently to ensure mixture does not stick to the pan.

At the end of the cooking time, approximately 2 hours, when the oil separates from the gravy, add sugar and stir constantly.

Allow meat to fry in the oily gravy until it is dark brown.

Serve with white rice and pineapple chutney or place Rendang on serving dish and arrange pineapple rings on top.

Note 1:   Heat 1 cup of milk (microwave milk for one minute) and mix with 2 tblsps coconut powder (Can substitute coconut milk if desired)

Note 2:   1 cup water heated in microwave, add 1 tblsp packaged tamarind, let it sit for a few minutes, strain and measure ½ cup

CHICKEN CURRY VASANTHICA

This is my mother's version of a Jaffna curry. When we immigrated to America forty three years ago, coconut products were scarce. Desiccated coconut and sweet coconut flakes used for baking were available at that time, so my mother started cooking with cow's milk and adding other products like evaporated milk to enhance the curry. Coconut powder came decades later. I have substituted coconut powder mixed with cow's milk in most of my recipes as fresh or canned coconut milk doesn't agree with me. This is a curry with lots of gravy and coconut milk is just as delicious in this recipe.

1	**3 to 3 ½ lb chicken, skinned & cut up with gizzards and liver**
1 tsp	**turmeric powder**
1 tsp	**salt**
¾ tsp	**chili powder**
1	**medium onion**
2 cloves	**garlic, sliced**
1 tsp	**chopped ginger**
4	**dried red chilies**
⅛ cup	**oil**
1 tsp	**black mustard seeds**
1 tsp	**cumin seeds**
1 med	**tomato, washed and patted dry, roughly chopped in large chunks**
1 tsp	**curry powder**
1 tsp	**fennel powder**
1 cup	**prepared coconut milk, see Note below**
1 tblsp	**evaporated milk, optional**
⅓	**fresh lime**

SERVING SIZE: 12 PREPARATION TIME: 1 HR 30 MINS

Mix cut up chicken with turmeric, chili powder and salt and leave aside.

Fry dried red chilies in hot oil. Add cumin and mustard seeds. When popped, add the garlic and fry for a few seconds.

Add the onions and then the ginger. When the onions are fried, add the chicken, and fry for 10 minutes.

Add tomato and fry for a few minutes, then cover and cook at medium heat for 20 minutes. Add more salt if required and the curry powder. Add fennel powder and cook for a few minutes. Pour coconut milk into the curry and cook on low heat.

Just before you take it off the fire, add a tblsp of evaporated milk for better flavor. Take curry off the heat and squeeze lime into the curry. Mix and leave aside until ready to serve.

Note: Heat 1 cup of milk (microwave milk for one minute) and mix with 2 tblsps coconut powder. (Can substitute coconut milk if desired)

CHILI EGGS

I love curries made with boiled eggs. In Sri Lanka we make a yellow curry and put the boiled eggs in it. We have another dish where you boil the eggs and deep fry after piercing, so that they don't burst and serve them in a spicy curry sauce. These chili eggs are part of an Indonesian Rijstaffel. The dishes served are Indonesian, but the rijsttafel's origins were colonial. During their presence in Indonesia, the Dutch introduced the rice table, not only so they could enjoy a wide array of dishes at a single setting, but also to impress visitors with the exotic abundance of their colony. Rijsttafels strive to feature an array of not only flavors and colors and degrees of spiciness but also textures, something not usually discussed in Western food.

4	eggs
3 tblsps	peanut oil
1 medium	onion, finely chopped
1 clove	garlic, crushed
½ tsp	dried shrimp flakes (blend small dried shrimp in food processor)
3 tsps	sambal olek or chili paste
½ tsp	Laos or galangal powder
3	kemiri (candle) or Brazil nuts, finely grated
½ tsp	salt
2 tsps	brown sugar
½ cup	coconut milk or ½ cup prepared coconut milk, see Note 1

SERVING SIZE: 8 PREPARATION TIME: 1 HOUR

Hard-boil the eggs. Heat oil in medium heat and fry onion and garlic until onion is soft and golden.

Add dried shrimp flakes, Sambal olek, Laos powder and grated nuts and fry for a few seconds.

Add salt, sugar, coconut milk and simmer gently, stirring constantly, until thick and oily in appearance about 10 to 15 minutes.

Shell and halve the eggs and place on a serving plate.

Spoon the sauce over them. Serve hot.

Note 1: Heat ½ cup of milk (microwave milk for one minute) and mix with 1 tblsp coconut powder.
Note 2: I have used peanuts in a pinch to replace Brazil or kemiri nuts.

CHILI CRABS OR PRAWNS

A very popular dish among my friends especially when it is made with crabs; Chili and black pepper crabs are very popular dishes in Singapore. The tourists and expats always frequented the restaurants in Boat Quay and the Seafood Center, close to the airport. But my Chinese colleagues, when I was living in Singapore in 2008 and some of the taxi drivers told me of an out of the way food stall where they cooked the best black pepper crab and, lo and behold!, it was in my neighborhood in Telok Kurau. The chili crabs were also superb but my favorite was the black pepper crabs.

I had an interesting experience one evening in Boat Quay after I had eaten chili crabs with some friends and went to pay the bill, I couldn't find my purse and was in a panic. My friends paid the bill of course, and I remembered that I had my purse at the famous Raffles Long Bar. I called them on the phone and the Security Officer confirmed that they had found it. When we got to the hotel the Security Officer had taken an inventory of every item in my purse right down to an American penny. He took out each item in front of me and checked the item on his list. Several of my friends have had similar experiences; Singapore is the safest city I have ever been to.

2 med.	raw Sri Lankan crabs OR
6 regular	Maryland blue crabs OR
1 ½ lb	large shrimp,
½ cup	peanut oil
3 cloves	garlic, finely chopped
2 tsps	finely grated fresh ginger
¼ cup	chili sauce
¼ cup	tomato ketchup
1 tblsp	sugar
1 tblsp	soy sauce
1 tsp	salt

SERVING SIZE: 6 PREPARATION TIME: 1 HOUR

Prepare crabs by removing shell cover, stomach and fibrous tissue, wash well and with cleaver, chop each crab into 2 pieces, or 4 pieces if they are large. If using shrimp leave the shells on.

Heat a wok to a medium high temperature, add oil, and when oil is very hot, fry the crab pieces until they change color, turning them so they cook on all sides for about 5 minutes.

Do not overcook, they must remain juicy inside.

If using shrimp fry until they just change color. Remove crabs or shrimp to a plate and drain with paper towels.

Turn heat to a low and fry the ginger, garlic, stirring constantly, until they are cooked but not brown. Mix the sauces, sugar, soy sauce and salt together and then add to wok and bring to a boil. Return crabs or shrimp to the wok and simmer in the sauce for 3 minutes.

Serve with white rice and a green vegetable such as Kai Lan (Chinese Broccoli).

LAMB CURRY VASANTHICA

This is by far my mother's best curry dish. I remember when we first arrived in Kuantan Malaysia. With much excitement we went to the wet market and the vendors in the stalls were grating coconuts and making fresh coconut milk. Of course we bought some and Amma, the Tamil name for mother, made us some delicious lamb curry which we "whacked", the term for enjoying a meal.

There is so much confusion in my mind about "mutton". In certain countries old sheep are called mutton and the young ones are called lamb. In Sri Lanka, goat meat is called mutton. In Jamaica and other Caribbean countries, a goat meat is called goat. I make this curry with both lamb and young goat which is very tender and delicious.

3 lbs	lamb shank, washed and cut in into 1 in. squares, ¼ in. thick
½ tsp	turmeric powder
1 tsp	salt
1 tblsp	margarine
2 cloves	garlic, chopped
1 tsp	ginger, chopped
1	cinnamon stick
4	cloves
1	small onion, chopped
1	small tomato, chopped
6	dry red chili peppers
½ tsp	fenugreek seed
½ tsp	black mustard seed,
½ tsp	cumin seed
1	large onion, sliced ⅛ inch thick
1 tblsp	margarine
½ tsp	chili powder (Sri Lankan)
1 tsp	curry powder
½ cup	prepared coconut milk, see Note below
⅛ cup	evaporated milk
1 tsp	fennel powder

SERVING SIZE: 12 PREPARATION TIME: 3 HOURS

Mix lamb with turmeric and salt, leave aside.

Melt 1 tblsp margarine in a large saucepan on high heat, add lamb and stir fry for 5 minutes. Add garlic, ginger, cinnamon stick, cloves, small chopped onion and tomato.

Lower heat to medium, cover and cook until meat is ¾ done about 40 minutes.

In the meantime in a different frying pan heat the remaining 1 tblsp margarine on medium high heat and fry the dry red chilies, fenugreek, mustard and cumin seeds. Then add sliced large onion and fry until glazed.

Add to lamb and cook covered for 2 minutes. Add chili powder and curry powder and cook covered until meat is boiled, about 15 minutes. Add coconut milk and cook uncovered until creamy, about 5 minutes. Add the evaporated milk and cook for another 5 minutes. Add fennel powder and cook until thickened, about 5 minutes)

Note: Heat ½ cup of milk (microwave milk for one minute) and mix with 1 tblsp coconut powder

OMELET CURRY

Recipe of my mother's, my favorite is Sunday breakfast with Kiri Bath (milk rice) and Lunu Miris (onion chili). This is a great rendition of the traditional omelet curry. Funnily enough, what comes to mind is that this was also my son's father's favorite meal. He was very close to my mother and spent many weeks at our home when I was traveling for work.

Growing up in the city of Colombo, we had a large coconut grove in the back of the house and it was full of cobras. As scared as I am of snakes, I used to play there until we found a cobra in the kitchen. Of course, the wet kitchens are usually in the back of the house and so was the hen house. The reason I started this story is to point out that my grandmother raised her own chickens that laid organic eggs as well as chickens to eat. My grandfather taught me how to kill chickens and clean them because the Buddhist and Hindu staff could not.

My father had great hopes that I would become a doctor someday. A surgeon no doubt, but I was better at math than memorizing data. I was a rebel who gave up biology for art to show my independence.

3	eggs		
2 tblsps	margarine or oil for making omelets	2 tsps	mustard seeds
CURRY GRAVY		½ tsp	salt
1	large onion, quartered and sliced	½ tsp	chili powder
1	large tomato, cut up into eighths	½ tsp	curry powder
¼ cup	oil	½ tsp	turmeric powder
4	dried red chili	1 ½ cups	milk
2 tsps	cumin seeds	2 tblsps	evaporated milk

SERVING SIZE: 6 PREPARATION TIME: 45 MINS

Make omelets by beating eggs first. Spread a little oil or margarine in a heated frying pan, when melted or hot, pour a small amount of beaten eggs and make thin omelets. Once cooked place omelets on a plate. Slice each omelet into three sections by cutting on the diagonal.

Heat oil in wok or frying pan over medium high heat until hot. Fry dried red chili, cumin and mustard and when mustard seeds start popping put onions and salt and fry.

When the onions are half done add tomatoes and continue frying. When tomatoes are ¾ fried add chili, turmeric and curry powders and continue to fry for a few minutes.

Pour milk into pan and boil. When milk is boiling, reduce heat, add egg omelets and cook on slow fire for a few minutes.

Just before taking it off the fire, add evaporated milk and heat.

RAAL SOTHI (WHITE PRAWN CURRY)

Recipe handed down by my loving grandmother Gertrude Philip. This is an original from their hometown in the island of Kayts. What I remember vividly is my grandmother being driven in the mornings to the beach in Karampan, our town on the island and sometimes she took me and my sister to await the fisherman coming in with their catch. She bought shrimp, prawns as we called it, and fresh fish.

Once she got home, she would make raal sothi for breakfast with our native dish called Puttu or String Hoppers and Pol Sambol (coconut sambal). We all sat down for breakfast at this long table that seated twenty people and, invariably, there were guests visiting our grandparents. Our grandparent's home, both in Karampan and Colombo was always filled with guests. In Kayts, they arranged for boats to take their guests to Fort Hammenheil which was in the middle of the ocean and the island of "Delft" whose wild ponies have been there for centuries. My grandparents were extremely hospitable people and they passed down these genes to their children and my sister Ramani and me.

½ tsp	turmeric powder	1 cup	milk
½ tsp	fenugreek seed	1 lb	medium fresh shrimp with shells and heads on
1	green chili pepper	1 tblsp	coconut powder
1	small onion, sliced 1/8 inch thick	⅛ cup	evaporated milk
1 tsp	salt	1 tsp	lime juice
¾ cup	water		

SERVING SIZE: 6 PREPARATION TIME: 30 MINUTES

Boil water with turmeric, onion, green chili, fenugreek and salt in a saucepan.
When onions are boiled, add milk and continue to boil.

When milk is boiling, add shrimp and let it cook. The shrimp must turn pink, about ten to fifteen minutes. If more gravy is needed add more milk.

Add the coconut powder and cook for three minutes. Add evaporated milk and cook for another two to three minutes. Take off fire and add lime juice and stir well.

SHRIMP CURRY, BRITISH RAJ

A recipe created by me while watching a travel channel, with cooking demonstrations of favorite dishes from famous hotels around the world, and this one was from the Raffles Hotel in Singapore. This dish was made for the British Raj during the colonial era as they couldn't take the spice, and the apples cut down the heat. It took me several failed attempts and a long time to perfect the recipe for the curry gravy.

My last outing with my mother was to spend a few days in Singapore during her visit to Malaysia in October, 1996. I was attending a course and she accompanied me there. My friend Ramola joined us in Singapore and we went for a special lunch at Raffles Hotel in the Tiffin room. We each had a Singapore sling made famous at Raffles and my mother told us how her father had brought her to Singapore fifty years ago when she was nineteen years old. He had bought her 50 saris and what it had been like in those days and how she had dined at this same restaurant.

Tiffin, referred as a light mid-day meal, has long been a Raffles tradition. Although tiffin curry has been served there since 1899, the main restaurant was named Tiffin Room in 1976. A restaurant run by the Sarkies the Armenian brothers who built the hotel and named it Raffles after Stamford Raffles, the founder of modern Singapore from the 1890s at Raffles Place was known as the Raffles Tiffin Rooms. For most of this century, a mild chicken curry was one of the few Asian mainstays on the hotel's daily menu as a Sunday tiffin curry was an essential aspect of colonial life.

6	**cloves garlic, chopped**
¼ cup	**oil**
1	**small can (4 oz) curry gravy for shrimp or seafood, Singapore curry gravy preferred**
3	**red delicious apples, peeled, cored and sliced**
1 ½ lb	**small or medium shrimp, peeled and deveined**

SERVING SIZE: 10 PREPARATION TIME: 45 MINUTES

Heat oil in wok over medium high heat until hot. Fry garlic in oil until golden, lower heat if garlic browns too easily as it should not burn. Add curry gravy and cook for a few minutes until it simmers.

Add sliced apples, mix and cook until soft.
Lastly add shrimp and cook until shrimp turns pink.
Do not overcook shrimp as it gets tough.

MUSTARD PRAWNS

A delicious shrimp curry from my mother's dear friend Savunthari Bastiampillai. Aunty Savunthari is also a great cook. I believe she harkens from an area called Negambo at some point in her life, where fresh seafood is in abundance as it is by the sea. They make the best crab curry, I am told. I learned to make crab curry from my mother and that, of course, came from my grandmother who cooked a good Thivu (island) curry, since they originated form Kayts. The mainland Jaffna folk, who are also from an island, call us the "island people". My dad's cousin and my special Uncle Rajan, explained it to me as "my dad was from the Mainland and my mother from the Island" and the combination was intriguing enough to make people wonder at their wedding.

1 lb shrimp, peeled and deveined	**SAUCE**
½ tsp turmeric powder	**1 ¼ tablespoons mustard seeds, ground**
1 tsp salt	**½ teaspoon chopped garlic**
½ tsp chili powder	**½ teaspoon chopped fresh ginger**
¼ cup oil	**¼ teaspoon sugar**
1 lb onion, sliced ⅛ inch thick	**½ teaspoon chili powder**
6 or 7 curry leaves	**⅓ teaspoon tamarind paste**
lime or lemon juice	

White vinegar,
Put all the ingredients above in a saucepan except the vinegar, pour enough vinegar to cover the rest of the ingredients and boil until the mixture thickens.

SERVING SIZE: 8 PREPARATION TIME: 45 MINUTES

Wash shrimp with a little lime or lemon juice and water and drain. Mix in turmeric, salt and chili powder.

Sauté shrimp in oil until the color changes. Add onions and sauté until golden brown, add curry leaves and fry for a few seconds.

Put all the SAUCE ingredients above in a saucepan except the vinegar, pour enough vinegar to cover the rest of the ingredients and boil until the mixture thickens.

2 tblsps coconut powder or coconut milk
1 tblsp tomato sauce, optional

Add the coconut milk or powder and tomato sauce and cook for a few seconds longer.
Place the shrimp and onion mixture in a serving bowl and cover with the sauce, mix and serve.

The bride's grandmother, the matriarch, Loku Archi greets the couple on their arrival to the reception with the traditional greeting, "Nameskaram!"

SIDE DISHES
RICE AND NOODLES

A staple in almost every country in Asia and cooked with an assortment of flavors.

One of my earliest recollections of Amma's cooking is her "Meehoon" dish made with rice sticks. She was fond of using chicken broth to make it into a wet noodle dish. For my part I have always preferred the dry noodle version.

MALAYSIAN CHINESE CHICKEN RICE

Recipe given to me by my Malaysian aunt, Angie Marshall, whose father was my grandfather's best friend and the two of them, immigrated to Malaya when Singapore and Malaysia were one country during Colonial times. My grandfather returned to Ceylon with his family, when my mother was seven years old. Several years after we moved to Maryland I was offered a job in Malaysia and I brought up the subject with my mother just before she went in for an eye operation. She laughingly told me that she was born in Malaysia and that perhaps she will die in Malaysia, which she did.

She also reintroduced me to Aunty Angie and assured me that I would not be alone in Malaysia. She said Aunty Angie would take care of me, and she certainly did. She still takes care of me. I love visiting Malaysia. I grew up with all these fascinating stories about Malaya and how beautiful the women were in their Kebaya, a national dress with a Sarong, which is like a wrap-around skirt and, in those times, a lace top, and she would describe the foods and the culture. I have grown to love Malaysia and consider it my adopted country.

In the beginning of 1996, while retired in Sri Lanka, my mother went back to the USA and visited all her friends in the Washington, DC, area and her very close friends in Boston, attended her niece Radhika's college graduation and visited with her sister and brother's family. Then in October, she came to Malaysia to see her grandson. That is the first thing she said when she got off the plane. She saw me often because I visited Sri Lanka very frequently, when my son was visiting his dad in New Jersey. She spent time teaching math to Michael Selvan and, two weeks later, she passed away in a hospital in Kuantan. Her prediction came true.

1 ½ cups	basmati or regular rice
½ whole	chicken cut into 2 inch pieces including bones
¼ tsp	salt
½ tsp	pepper
⅛ cup	soy sauce (light or regular)
⅛ cup	dark soy sauce
¼ tsp	sesame oil
½ bulb	garlic, peeled and smashed or sliced
½ lb	mushrooms or 1 can of mushrooms, sliced
2 small	onions sliced thin
½ cube	chicken stock
⅛ cup	oil
8 slices	crystallized ginger
1 ½ to 2 ¼	cups boiling water, 1 ½ cups for Basmati & 2 ¼ cups for Regular long grain rice

SERVING SIZE: 8 PREPARATION TIME: 1 HR 30 MIN

Marinade chicken in light and dark soy sauce, bit of salt, pepper and a little sesame oil for 3 hours.

Heat oil in wok over medium high heat, add garlic and onions. When half fried, add chicken and fry for 10 minutes.

Cover and fry for about 20 minutes until ¾ cooked. Add rice in wok and fry for a few minutes. Add mushrooms. Take out and put in rice cooker with ½ cube of chicken stock dissolved in boiling water.

For regular rice add 2 ¼ cups water; for basmati rice 1 ½ cups of water.

Place crystallized ginger slices on top and turn on rice cooker. Serve as a one pot meal.

INDONESIAN FRIED RICE

A mouthwatering rice dish from my sister but given to me by our mother. Ramani got this recipe from an Indonesian lady who babysat her daughter Shivani, when she was little. In Indonesia this dish is called "Nasi Goreng". Nasi means rice and Goreng means fried.

Growing up in Sri Lanka, I didn't get to meet too many people from other countries. However, one of my classmates in school happened to be the daughter of an Indonesian diplomat and I got invited to their house for her birthday parties. I found the food to be delicious.

As an adult I had the opportunity to eat Indonesian food when I was visiting Aruba. I found an Indonesian restaurant on a boat and they served a Rijstafel. Later on, the Indonesian consulate in New York had a restaurant that served Indonesian food, which I frequented very often when I was living in Roselle Park, New Jersey, where Michael Selvan was born. After they closed that restaurant, I missed the food so much I started teaching myself to cook Indonesian food and, finally, progressed to making the Rijstafel.

2 cups	rice, cooked & cooled
3 cloves	garlic, peeled & chopped
1 large	onion, peeled and sliced
1 bunch	scallions, washed & patted dry, sliced ½ inch thick
½ cup	vegetable oil
1 lb	chicken (optional), skinned and boned, cut into small pieces
1 lb	shrimp (optional), cleaned, deveined and halved
1 large	tomato, washed and patted dry, chopped
2 tblsps	sambal olek
⅛ cup	Kecap Manis (Indonesian sweet soy sauce)

SERVING SIZE: 8 PREPARATION TIME: 1 HOUR

Mix shrimp with ½ tsp salt. Marinate chicken or mix with a ½ tsp soy sauce.

Heat oil in a wok over medium high heat until hot. Add onions and garlic, stir fry and then push aside, add scallions. Fry for a minute and push aside to the rim of the wok.

Add chicken and fry until cooked. Push aside, add shrimp and cook until shrimp turns pink.

Add sambal olek and continue to fry for 2 or 3 minutes.
Mix everything and push aside. Add tomatoes and cook.
When tomatoes are cooked add 1 tblsp sweet soy sauce and mix.

Add cooked rice and mix. Let cook for 3 minutes until rice is mixed and absorbs all the flavors. Add remainder of the soy sauce, mix and taste. Add more soy sauce if required.

Note: This dish can be completely vegetarian by omitting the shrimp and chicken. To make sweet soy sauce if Kecap Manis is not available add some dark soy, some soy sauce and brown sugar or palm sugar and mix.

KIRI BATH (MILK RICE) & KATTA SAMBAL

My mother's version of this dish goes well with the Omelet Curry. Kiri bath is made by some using red rice and with country rice by the Singhalese. My mom puts sugar in it, which I love, but people tend to think it is odd because, traditionally, Sri Lankans do not add sugar. The Singhalese serve this dish with a sour fish called Ambulthiyal. Generally, we end our New Year's Eve parties eating Kiri Bath, Katta Sambol or Lunu Miris and Ambulthiyal at 4 A.M., on New Year's Day.

2 cups	regular rice, washed and drained
3 ½ cups	water
½ tsp	salt
1 ½ cups	milk
¼ cup	sugar

SERVING SIZE: 8 PREPARATION TIME: 30 MINS

Put the rice, salt and water in a large saucepan and bring to a boil. Cover and cook on a very low fire. When ¾ of the water has evaporated, add the milk and sugar and mix the rice.

Cover and continue to cook until rice is cooked and all liquids are absorbed (about 20 minutes.)

Put rice on a plate to a height of 1 ½ inches and trace diamond shapes on top of the rice, but don't cut all the way through until ready to serve.

Serve with store bought Lunu Miris or homemade Katta Sambal.
(See recipe below:)

KATTA SAMBAL

1 large	red (Bermuda) onion, grated. Cut up the rest of the onion.
½ tsp	chili powder
½ tsp	salt
½ tsp	Maldive fish (available in Sri Lankan grocery stores)
½	lime

Squeeze water from the onion, and then add chili powder and salt to taste.

Start with ½ tsp chili powder and salt. Add Maldives fish and mix then add lime and mix.

Note: Kiri Bath served with Katta Sambal and Omelet curry is a great combination for breakfast or special occasions.

The "Koorai" sari being blessed by the guests.

VEGETABLE BURIYANI PARSI

Recipe given to my mother by her best friend Dr. Shera Samaraweera, who is also very special to me and I loved her dearly. Aunty Shera, as I fondly called her, was a big influence in my life. She would always wear these light colored pastel saris and it fascinated me. My mom wore traditional saris, which were darker in color. I find that I wear mostly pastel colors and love the saris that have a Parsi look with beaded work and soft materials.

Aunty Shera was from the Parsi community of Sri Lanka. They came to Sri Lanka from North India. Their ancestors are from what was formerly called Persia and now Iran. The Persians were Zoroastrians, not Moslems, like the current population. Zorro's was the Persian prophet and founder of Zoroastrianism. They have some interesting burial customs that caught my attention and fascinate me.

3 or 4	green chilies			
2 tblsps	cumin seed		2 tblsps	vegetable oil
2 tblsps	curry powder		8 ozs	yogurt
1 ½ x 1 in.	piece of ginger		1 tsp	salt

SERVING SIZE: 8 PREPARATION TIME: 45 MINS

Grind the 4 ingredients above in a blender or food processor with a bit of water.

Heat oil in a frying pan over medium heat until hot. Add mixture and fry for a few minutes and then put yogurt and boil for a few more minutes. Add salt and set aside.

1 large	onion
½ stick	butter (4 tblsps)
1 small	tomato, washed and patted dry, cut up into chunks
2 cups	basmati rice, washed and drained and mixed with ½ tsp turmeric
4 cups	cold water, more if required

Melt the butter in a large saucepan over medium heat, add onions and fry. When onions are ¼ fried add tomato and continue frying until half done. Put rice in pan and fry for 5 minutes.

In the meantime, put yogurt mixture into a 4 cup measuring cup and add enough cold water to make 4 cups of liquid.

Add to the rice, when it is boiling lower heat to low, cover and simmer until all liquid has evaporated.

Serve in a dish and garnish with fried onions or sliced boiled eggs.

COLD-SPICY SESAME NOODLES

I see this dish at many buffet lunches in the Washington, DC, area in food places mostly owned by Koreans. Sometimes they add snow peas, red peppers, carrots and other vegetables. I prefer it plain as described below. This dish is served cold and is great with baked ham or served as an accompaniment in the same manner as a salad.

1 lb	linguine or thin spaghetti
2 tblsps	sesame oil
1 tblsp	fresh ginger root, minced
4 tsps	sugar
¼ cup	soy sauce
¼ cup	peanut butter
2 tblsps	wine vinegar
¼ tsp	red pepper flakes (optional)
2 stalks	scallion, cut into ¼ inch pieces

SERVING SIZE: 10 PREPARATION TIME: 1 HOUR

Cook linguine according to label directions; drain.
Toss with sesame oil and refrigerate until cold.

In a small bowl combine ginger with remaining ingredients except scallions and mix with a wire whisk or chops sticks.

Pour over chilled noodles and toss until well coated.

Sprinkle scallions on top. Refrigerate until ready to serve.

MEEHOON (RICE NOODLES)

My mom used to make this dish with lots of chicken stock and it was a wet noodle dish. I prefer the dry noodles and, through trial and error, I created this dish. I first tasted the dried sausage in a noodle dish at a restaurant in Kuantan. It was a small restaurant that served some original dishes such as stir fried vegetables with eggplant, green beans, onions and salted fish.

In Sri Lanka, they serve a Meehoon dish with various curries in place of rice. It is generally vegetarian, not to take away from the flavor of the meat and seafood curries.

In Singapore, they call the Meehoon dish "Singapore Noodles" which is flavored with curry powder and turmeric to make it spicy and yellow in color.

1 pkg	**Meehoon (thin rice sticks)**
4 to 5 cups	**water**

SERVING SIZE: 8 PREPARATION TIME: 1 HOUR

Some rice sticks from the Asian stores have 3 packs in 1 package. Use only 2 packs from these packages.

Boil 4 to 5 cups water in a large saucepan. Turn off water and put rice sticks in the water for 3 minutes.

Remove from water and drain. Let cool.

This can be done ahead, covered and refrigerated. If it is done all at once place, drained rice sticks in the freezer to cool while you prepare the other ingredients.

½ cup	oil
3 large	cloves garlic
1 med	onion, sliced
2	bunches of scallion
8	Chinese dried mushrooms soaked in hot water for 15 minutes. Dry with a paper towel and slice
2	carrots, grated or sliced like matchsticks
½ lb	small shrimp, optional, peeled and deveined, coat with ½ tsp cornstarch and ½ tsp salt
2	eggs, beaten, add salt and pepper to taste
⅛ cup	soy sauce
4	Chinese dried sausage, optional
1 small	chicken breast or red meat diced into little pieces and mixed with a little soy sauce, optional

Slice the sausage into thin slices and fry with no oil in a small frying pan.

Remove from fire and drain on paper towels.

Heat oil in wok over medium high heat, add garlic and then the onions a few seconds later. When half fried, add scallions in the middle of the wok and fry for a few seconds. Push scallions, onion and garlic to the sides of the wok, add mushrooms and carrots to the side of the wok.

Add the chicken to the center of the wok and fry for several minutes until cooked, push chicken to the side and add shrimp and fry until shrimp turns pink. Push shrimp to the side.

Add beaten eggs to center of pan and scramble for a few minutes. Add rice sticks and mix with fork or toss to mix, add soy sauce and mix all ingredients. Continue frying until well mixed about 5 to 8 minutes.

Serve in a dish garnished with the slices of Chinese sausage on top.

Note: Instead of adding beaten eggs to the meehoon while cooking, make thin omelets in a small frying pan and slice into thin strips and garnish when serving. Ground peanuts go well as a garnish too.

SHRIMP BURIYANI

This unusual recipe was given to me by my neighbor in Toms River, New Jersey, over twenty five years ago, by Nita Pradhan, who was raised near a coastal town in India close to Bombay now called Mumbai. Everyone makes Biryani or Buriyani but mostly, Chicken and Lamb. In Sri Lanka, the Muslims make fantastic Buriyani.

Twenty five years ago when I started making this dish it was unusual to find seafood Buriyani. I was very lucky to have known the Pradhans. They were wonderful neighbors. This dish is loved by my friends from various parts of the world.

MARINADE		RICE	
1 lb	shrimp, peeled and deveined	3 cups	basmati rice washed and drained
1 tsp	fresh ginger root, chopped	4½ cups	water
1 large	clove garlic, chopped	4	cardamom seeds
¼ cup	tamarind	4	cloves
½ tsp	turmeric powder	1	cinnamon stick
½ tsp	chili powder	1 cup	frozen small peas, thawed and drained
1 tsp	salt	¼ cup	fried onions
1 large	onion		

SERVING SIZE: 8 PREPARATION TIME: 2 HR

Marinade shrimp with the remaining 6 ingredients for 1 hour or more. I marinate this overnight.

Slice the onion thin, deep fry in oil, drain on paper towels and set aside.

Cook rice in a rice cooker with the ingredients mentioned above.

BURIYANI MIXTURE

4 oz	**packet of frozen or fresh grated coconut**
½ cup	**chopped coriander (cilantro) leaves**
1 or 2	**green chilies, chopped**
3 tblsps	**oil**
1 med	**onion, chopped**
3 tblsps	**oil**

Mix grated coconut coriander and green chilies together in a small bowl.

Fry coconut mixture in 3 tblsps oil, drain and keep separately. If there is no oil left in the pan add the 3 more tblsps of oil and when hot add onions and fry for about 5 minutes until transparent. Add shrimp with marinade and cook over medium heat. When shrimp turns pink and is cooked, add coconut mixture and mix.

Assemble Buriyani

In a glass or ceramic oval, square or rectangular dish, layer the buriyani by adding a layer of rice, shrimp mixture on top of it and then sprinkling one third of the remaining fried onions. Continue layering one more time and ending with the fried onions as a garnish on top. Use extra coriander leaves for garnish to give it a pretty look.

Note: This dish served with Eggs & Onion Sambol (pg. 82) and some Mango Chutney is a great combination.

VEGETABLES

Amma's first attempt at fusion was substituting Western vegetables in her curries.

The bane of Amma's existence was her two daughters she had trouble feeding as children. We ate bland curries without any chili powder and the only vegetables I ate were carrots, potatoes and cabbage. My mother would chase me around the house in an attempt to feed me.

AMBROSIA SALAD

A dish favored by most of my mother's friends, both in the USA and Sri Lanka. Whenever I am in Sri Lanka, my mother's relatives and friends, speak about this dish and how delicious it was. It is a light, cooling dish, especially in tropical countries and great for a buffet.

1 large	can (30 oz) of fruit cocktail
1 can (8 oz)	pineapple chunks
½ cup	raisins
2	apples
1 cup	grapes
½ cup	vanilla yogurt
½ cup	mayonnaise
¼ cup	sweet coconut flakes

SERVING SIZE: 16 PREPARATION TIME: 20 MIN

Drain the fruit cocktail and the pineapple chunks. Mix fruit together and add the raisins.

Put cut up apples and grapes into the mixture above. Add vanilla yogurt and mayonnaise.

Lastly mix in shredded sweet coconut. Put in a bowl and serve cold.

BROCCOLI AND CHEESE CASSEROLE

Gail Stern, my first and oldest friend in the USA gave me this appetizing vegetable casserole for a party buffet. We ended up as sisters-in-law as we married two brothers and our children are first cousins. When I graduated college, Gail, our friend Brett, whose parents were family friends of our in-laws and I went on a three week road trip. We went from Boston to North Carolina and onwards to California, from Los Angeles to San Francisco and back through Utah to Boston.

On our way to Los Angeles, we stopped at a bar in Little Rock, Arkansas. It was frightening for me, as I don't think they had ever seen a person of color with straight hair; in other words, from my part of the world. We were very bold in 1975. There were times when we were very hungry, as we ran out of money and had to wait until one of our parents wired us some. We camped most of the way and, sometimes, we slept in rest areas. I remember how safe it was in those days. Three women in this day and age would find it dangerous to do the same road trip we did.

2	packages (10 oz) chopped frozen broccoli
2	eggs, beaten
½ cup	milk
¾ cup	mayonnaise
2 cups	sharp cheddar cheese, grated
½ cup	or ½ lb mushrooms, sliced
1 can	cream of celery soup
1 tsp	Worcestershire sauce
1 tblsp	chopped onion

SERVING SIZE: 8 PREPARATION TIME: 1 HR

Pre-heat the oven to 350°F. Cook and drain the broccoli.

Mix all ingredients together in the same dish that will be used to cook in such as a square or oval glass baking dish.

Cover with foil and bake for 40 minutes or sprinkle cracker crumbs on top and bake uncovered.

CORN SALAD

This flavorful dish is from my sister's friend Joey Campbell, who got it from her mother, Mrs. Campbell. I make it every year for my Christmas buffet. It is a very colorful dish with Christmas colors and easy to make.

The other day I was in Dallas, Texas, on a business trip, and I was taken to dinner at a famous steak place in Richardson by my hosts and I ordered a burnt corn salad. It was similar to mine with peppers and tomatoes but the corn was burnt a bit as they used corn on the cob that had been cooked in a barbecue and taken off the Cobb. So, adventurous cooks can try this, especially in countries where you can't get canned corn.

2 cans (15 oz)	**white or yellow corn or 1 yellow and 1 white, drained**
2	**scallions, cut into ¼ inch pieces**
1	**green or red pepper, cut into little pieces**
1	**tomato, diced**
1 tblsp	**Italian salad dressing**
1 tblsp	**mayonnaise**
1 tsp	**sugar**

SERVING SIZE: 12 PREPARATION TIME: 30 MINS

Mix the corn, cut vegetables and toss with mayonnaise, Italian salad dressing and sugar.

Put in a bowl and serve.

Note: Great for festive occasions like Christmas as this dish adds lots of color to the table.

SAMMY'S POTATO SALAD

My dear friend Sammy Gail Johnson gave me this yummy potato salad. She transitioned from making authentic southern food to healthy food. Going back to my business trip to Dallas, I had the pleasure of being served Southern barbecue for lunch and my hosts, as well as my coworker, Willie, all Southerners, told me stories of how their mothers cooked certain foods, okra, in particular.

In Sri Lanka we make okra as a sautéed dry curry but, in the South, they batter fry okra, and it is delicious. But one of them told me his mother dipped the cut okra in plain old cornmeal and deep fried it. They told me stories of shrimp boils and other foods their mothers made and I was completely fascinated.

I am a foodie and love learning about the different foods of other countries and regions. I remember being in Portugal and eating the foods of the Algarve region, especially the Seafood Cataplana, made in a special copper pan that looks like a closed clam.

2 lbs	potatoes, washed peeled and cut up into large cubes
¼ tsp	celery seeds
1 ¼	tsps sweet relish
½ tsp	mustard
3 tblsps	mayonnaise
5 tblsps	onions, chopped
¾ tsps	salt
¼ tsp	black pepper
1	boiled egg, cut up

SERVING SIZE: 8 PREPARATION TIME: 45 MINS

Boil potatoes in large sauce pan with enough water to cover them. Making sure the potatoes are soft but not overcooked. Remove from heat and drain. Mix all ingredients together while potatoes are still hot.

Place in a serving dish and chill. Garnish with another boiled egg and parsley.

EGGPLANT–AGGIE

A tasty eggplant dish from Aggie Nona, my Mom's helper, when she retired to Sri Lanka in December, 1994. Aggie was Singhalese and taught my mother a few of their recipes. Aggie worked for my grand aunt Grace, and then for her daughter, Vaneetha, and family, before they immigrated to the USA. Aggie died several years ago and is fondly remembered and loved by all who knew her.

3 small	long thin eggplants, sliced thin.
½ tsp	turmeric powder
¼ tsp	salt
½ med	red onion, sliced thin
1	green chili, sliced thin
¼ tsp	salt
¼	of a lime

SERVING SIZE: 1 PREPARATION TIME: 30 MINUTES

Vegetable oil for frying.

Mix eggplant salt and turmeric. Fry pieces of eggplant in hot vegetable oil and drain on paper towels.

Mix onion, green chili, salt and lime by hand and squeezing onion so it is well mixed with remaining ingredients.

Add eggplants mix lightly and serve.

MUSHROOM CURRY

Nira Sathiakumaran, my mother loved her as a daughter. I used to jokingly say to my mother that Nira was a better daughter than we were. She loved my mother and was devoted to her and helped her out in enormous ways. Our sons were born around the same time, separated by a year, and grew up together in their early years, before we went off to Malaysia.

Since mushrooms were not native to Sri Lanka, this dish created by Nira was done by adapting our cooking methods to new vegetables.

1 lb	sliced mushrooms or whole mushrooms washed, patted dry and sliced
1 ½ tblsps	oil
½ med	onion, sliced thin
2 cloves	garlic, sliced thin
½ tsp	chili powder
1 tsp	curry powder
½ tsp	salt
⅛ cup	prepared coconut milk, see Note below

SERVING SIZE: 6 PREPARATION TIME: 30 MINUTES

Cut up mushrooms. Heat oil in a frying pan over medium heat until hot. Add garlic and onions and sauté for 3 minutes. Add mushrooms and mix. Lower heat, add chili, curry powder, and salt and cook on a low fire until mushrooms are cooked. As the mushrooms cook they shrink and generate a lot of gravy. Add the coconut milk and cook until boiling.

Note : Heat ⅛ cup of milk (microwave milk for one minute) and mix with ½ tsp coconut powder

PUMPKIN CURRY

A tasty curry using Asian pumpkin made by Aggie, a Malaysian Indian lady, who worked for my friends Lyn and Chris and, then, helped me out, when I was stationed in Kuantan. She always served food at her house on a banana leaf and it brought back memories of eating on banana leaves at family weddings in the island of Kayts.

I also remember this hilarious story of how everyone sat down to eat at my parents wedding lunch which was served on banana leaves with no utensils. Once the meal is served the guests can't eat until the bride and groom start eating. Unfortunately, my dad would not start eating, so my grandparents thought, he wanted more money for the dowry and they went to their bedroom "Almara" same as Armoire and a wardrobe and brought out money and gave it to him. He still didn't eat.

This continued for some time with my grandparents bringing more presents out and, finally, in a sheepish voice, he asks for a fork and spoon, as he never ate with his fingers. We used to call him the brown Englishman.

3 lbs	Asian pumpkin, peeled and cut into large cubes	1 tsp	cumin powder
		1 tsp	salt
2 large	cloves garlic, sliced	½ to 1 tsp	chili powder
1 inch	ginger, chopped	⅛ cup	oil
1 med	onion, sliced	1 cup	prepared coconut milk, see Note below
8	curry leaves	1 cup	water
1 tsp	mustard seeds	½ tsp	sugar

SERVING SIZE: 8 PREPARATION TIME: 1 HOUR

Heat oil in a large saucepan over medium heat until hot. Add garlic, ginger, onion, curry leaves, mustard seeds, cumin powder, and chili powder and sauté for about 15 minutes.

Put pumpkin cubes, salt, water and sugar into pan. Bring to a boil and cook covered for about 30 minutes. When pumpkin is cooked add the coconut milk and cook for 5 minutes.

Note: Heat 1 cup of milk (microwave for 1 minute) and mix with 2 tblsps coconut powder. (Can substitute coconut milk if desired)

BLACK PEPPER GREEN BEANS

One of my mother's signature dishes that Aggie Nona taught her. A Singhalese dish that is very peppery and delicious, and looks more like a salad called a "Mallung". The black pepper adds a great flavor to green bean curries. My friend Shyama told me that the Singhalese from the Southern part of the island use a lot of black pepper instead of red chili in their curries. The island of Sarawak, in East Malaysia, is famous for its black pepper.

2 tsp	black pepper seeds
2 tsp	cumin seeds
2 tsp	mustard seeds
1 large	onion, chopped
⅓ cup	oil
2 lbs	fresh green beans, cleaned and cut into bite size ¼ to ½ inch pieces
1 tsp	turmeric powder
1 ½ tsp	salt
2 cloves	garlic
⅔ cup	fresh or frozen coconut

SERVING SIZE: 12 PREPARATION TIME: 45 MINUTES

Blend black pepper and cumin seeds in a food processor or mortar and pestle.

Heat oil in a wok or a deep frying pan over medium heat until hot. Fry mustard seeds and onion until mustard seeds pop.

Mix turmeric and salt with beans and add to onions. Cover and cook until half done (sprinkle with water if it gets dry).

Pound garlic with a mortar and pestle or the back of a knife. Mix garlic with coconut, and black pepper, cumin mix.

Uncover beans and add coconut mixture to beans and mix.

Take beans off the fire put in dish and serve.

Guests enjoyuing the wedding lunch surrounded by palm trees.

SAMBOLS & CHUTNEYS

The only way Amma could make my sister and I eat rice and curry was by adding chutney or a sambol with dusting of sugar. People always think it odd when we add sugar to our Pol (coconut) sambol as we are the only Sri Lankans that seem to do this.

EGGS & ONION SAMBOL

A great side dish for a Sri Lankan buffet table or to serve with Biryani. My mom's buffet table was scrumptious. She could never stop at a few dishes, and they were elaborately arranged. She always taught us, not only to serve tasty dishes, but also to arrange beautiful table settings with fresh flowers and candles. She gave me a book on different ways to fold napkins and one on making different shapes with raw vegetables. My sister and I take great pride in entertaining — a tribute to our Mom.

8	eggs, hard boiled and cooled
1 med	red onion, sliced very thin
½ tsp	salt
½ tsp	chili powder
½ small	lime

SERVING SIZE: 8 PREPARATION TIME: 20 MINUTES

Remove shells and slice eggs and arrange on a platter.

Mix onion, salt and chili powder and then squeeze the lime into this mixture, as explained below.

Squeeze half the piece of lime first, mix by hand, taste and if it requires more, then squeeze the rest of the piece of lime.

This dish has to be mixed by hand for the onion to absorb the rest of the ingredients.

Spread the onion mixture on top of the eggs and serve.

EGGPLANT & YOGURT SAMBOL

Some call this dish an eggplant pachadi, a raw salad and while it is a popular dish in Indian and Sri Lankan cuisine this one created by my mother tastes different. The eggplant is roasted and, together with the yogurt, makes this a healthy dish and reminds me of Egypt.

I had to give a presentation to the Suez Canal authorities and was lucky enough to get an extra day in with my colleague, Courtney. After our presentation we had some free time and the local agent arranged for us to go to the Giza pyramids, together with his security officer.

During our visit at Giza some camel drivers talked us into renting camels for $50 per hour to go shopping. Each of us had a camel driver who rode on the camel with us and would race across the dessert from the Pyramids to the shops. Our agent was upset because he thought the price was too high and the Security Officer had let them rip us off but it was exciting; and going shopping on a camel was cool.

1 large	eggplant
½ tblsp	oil
1 med	red onion, sliced very thin
½ tsp	salt
1	green chili, sliced
¼ small	lime
½ – ¾ cup	yogurt

SERVING SIZE: 8 PREPARATION TIME: 1 HR 15 MINS

Preheat oven to 350°F.

Coat eggplant with oil using a basting brush or your hands. Bake in oven for about one hour.

The skin must be withered. If it is still purple, cook it longer.

Mix onion, salt and chili pieces and then squeeze the lime into this mixture. Mix by hand squeezing the onions as you mix.

This dish has to be mixed by hand for the onion to absorb the rest of the ingredients.

Remove the pulp from the eggplant (throw out the peels and as much of the seeds as you can. The seeds can be removed as one.), place in a small bowl and smash until smooth.

Add to onion mixture and mix with a spoon or by hand. Put in a dish and serve.

INDONESIAN CHUTNEY

Truly divine chutney made by my mother which had a life of its own. My mother gave this recipe to several people, including me, and the ingredient for the hot and spicy flavor varied with each individual.

Indonesia reminds me of Bali. On a flight back to Malaysia from Australia, I looked down from my window seat and I could clearly see the volcano in Bali, with smoke billowing out of it and I took a picture of it and it was spectacular. Michael Selvan and I saw the "Ramayana" danced in an outdoor theater in Bali just after I had given him the book to read. Bali is primarily Hindu, as opposed to other parts of Indonesia, which are Moslem.

This chutney goes well with fried rice, noodles, hamburgers and vegetarian dishes. I once tried it on a slice of cooked Turkish sausage, with my scrambled eggs.

1 ½ cups	white vinegar
1 ½ cups	sugar
1 tblsp	chili sauce or 2 tsps red pepper flakes
3 large	red bell peppers
5 cloves	garlic
½ cup	sultanas or golden raisins

SERVING SIZE: 2 GLASS BOTTLES (16OZ) PREPARATION TIME: 1 HR 20 MINS

Cut pepper into small pieces after seeding.

Mix all ingredients in a large saucepan and bring to boil. Lower the heat and cook on a slow fire for 1 hour.

Let the chutney cool in the pan. Put it in a food processor and blend.

Store the chutney in a sterilized bottle.

PINEAPPLE CHUTNEY

Yummy chutney I picked up along the way. In Sri Lanka, they make a salad out of fresh cut pineapple with salt, hot chili powder and vinegar or mixed with plain old Asian chili sauce. Growing up and going to school in what was then Ceylon, we ate pineapple like folks eat watermelon slices in the USA. They were a healthy snack along with fresh mangoes, many varieties of bananas, papaya and guava. This chutney goes well with pork dishes and an accompaniment to Beef Rendang.

1	pineapple, peeled, cored and crushed in a food processor
1 ½ cups	sugar
1 tsp	salt
1	lemon, squeezed and the juice extracted
1 ½ tsp	fennel seeds
1 ½ tsp	cumin seeds
½ tsp	chili powder
½ tsp	ground pepper
1 tsp	black pepper seeds

SERVING SIZE : 2 GLASS BOTTLES (16OZ) PREPARATION TIME: 1 HOUR

Place the pineapple, sugar, salt and lemon juice in a non aluminum saucepan and cook on medium high heat for about 30 minutes, stirring constantly so that it does not boil over. When it has reached the consistency of a jam, take off the fire and cool to room temperature.

In a small food processor or a mortar and pestle, coarsely grind the fennel and cumin seeds and mix in with the pineapple.

Add the chili powder and both black peppers.

Cover the saucepan and place in a cool place for 1 week. Keep away from the sun.

Store the chutney in a sterilized bottle.

DESSERTS & CAKES

Amma's famous signature dish was Sticky Toffee Pudding that entices even non–dessert lovers.

My parents moved to England shortly after they were married as my father was to take an Army Officer's Training Course there. I was conceived in England and before Amma returned to Sri Lanka for her confinement my parents spent some time on holiday in Europe. Their travels included France, Italy and Germany among other countries and I attribute my "Wanderlust" to these small beginnings.

CHOCOLATE BISCUIT PUDDING

A popular Sri Lankan dessert I stumbled upon and liked the fact that the egg yolks are cooked. Several versions of this recipe are made with raw egg yolks. Chocolate biscuit pudding is very popular in the dessert buffets at different hotels in various parts of Sri Lanka. My brother-in-law Kumar's sister, used to make it for him with the original Kandos chocolate. I like it with Cadbury's milk chocolate. This is an easy dessert to make anywhere in the world because Marie or Maria biscuits are available everywhere.

4	egg yolks (no whites)
1 cup	milk
4 squares	(1 oz per square) cooking chocolate, see Note below
½ cup	chopped cashews
8 ozs	butter, cut up for easier beating
1 tsp	vanilla
¾ lb	confectionaries sugar (sifted)
1 pkg	(7oz) of Marie Biscuits
½ cup	milk

SERVING SIZE: 8 PREPARATION TIME: 45 MINUTES

Beat egg yolks and milk. Cook in a double boiler until it becomes custard (it thickens and coats a wooden spoon) and then remove from the fire.

Melt chocolate in custard and add vanilla and mix. Place butter in a mixing bowl, pour the custard into butter and beat for about 5 minutes. Add the sifted confectioners sugar and beat until creamy. Add the chopped cashews and mix with a spatula.

Dip each Marie (also known as Maria in Hispanic food stores) biscuit in milk and place in a dish to cover the bottom. Put in a layer of the custard cream and repeat the layer of biscuits and cream.

Top with a few cashew halves for decoration and refrigerate.

Leave the pudding out for about 5 to 10 minutes before serving.

Note: Cadbury or Ghirardelli milk or Kandos (Sri Lankan) chocolate can be used for this recipe. The Ghirardelli was delicious and so was the Cadbury chocolate.

MANGO MOUSSE

A heavenly dessert created by me. When I first tasted this dish made by a very dear friend it was delicious but too soft. While recreating this dish, I stumbled upon a strawberry mousse recipe, in the back of a box of superfine sugar. I adapted it to make this mousse. It is very popular among my friends.

Mango mousse makes me think of the Raffles Hotel in Singapore. The bakery café makes all kinds of tropical mousses, including mango and passion fruit. I enjoyed sitting outside at the café having tea with scones and jam watching the shoppers go in and out of the mall next door. People watching is something I enjoy very much.

1 can	Mango puree (30 oz)
1 tblsp	gelatin
⅓ cup	water
1 ½ cups	heavy cream
½ cup	superfine sugar
2	egg whites
2 tblsps	superfine sugar
1	mango (or 1 kiwi), skinned and sliced, optional

SERVING SIZE: 12 PREPARATION TIME: 45 MINUTES

In a small saucepan, sprinkle gelatin over water and let stand till softened. Heat until gelatin dissolves.

Put mango in a mixing bowl and add the gelatin and beat until blended, less than 5 minutes.

Beat cream with ½ cup of sugar until soft peaks form. Fold mango puree into cream.

Beat egg whites until foamy. Gradually add 2 tblsp sugar and continue beating until stiff.

Do not overbeat as it will be hard to fold the eggs into the mango cream.

Fold egg whites into the mango cream.

Place in a pretty bowl and garnish with sliced mangoes or kiwi.

PAVLOVA

A scrumptious recipe given to me by an Aussie colleague when I was working for "COMSAT", a company I loved. My son and I traveled to Australia before I returned to the USA from Malaysia.

Pavlova reminds me of the tour we took from Sydney to the Three Sisters, which are three sandstone rock formations in the Blue Mountains seven in all. We saw the most colorful parrots, flying around us as we climbed down and for a novice birder like me, it was paradise. Afterwards, we had lunch in a park and the guide taught twelve year old Michael Selvan how to throw a boomerang. We enjoyed eating lamingtons for the first time, and other Australian delicacies and on the way back, we stopped for tea and I had pavlova for the first time.

MERINGUE		TOPPING	
6	egg whites	1 cup	whipping or heavy cream
	pinch salt	¼ to ½ cup	sugar
1 ¾	cups caster or superfine sugar	Fresh fruits cut up such as apples, mangoes,	
2 tsps	white vinegar	kiwi, strawberries and blueberries.	
1 tsp	vanilla		

SERVING SIZE: 12 PREPARATION TIME: 2 HOURS

Preheat oven to 250°F.

Combine egg whites, salt and beat until firm shiny pears form.
Gradually beat in about ¾ of sugar and continue to beat until stiff and glossy. Fold in vinegar, vanilla and remaining sugar.

Cut out a 12 inch circle of baking or brown (wax) paper.
Spoon on the egg mixture onto the paper and make about a 10 inch round.

Bake in center of oven until crisp on the outside and just set in the center for 1 ¼ to 1 ½ hours. Remove and carefully invert onto serving plate, and cool.

TOPPING

Beat the cream with the sugar on high speed until soft peaks form.

Put a layer of whipped cream on meringue using a spoon and put the fresh fruits on top and dot with whipped cream and serve.

TIRAMISU

My friend Chemi gave me the recipe for this luscious dessert. Tiramisu reminds me of my Italian trip I planned on the Internet. My Aunt Vaneetha and I spent two nights in a basic Bed & Breakfast outside Rome and took the metro every morning to see Vatican City, the Coliseum and the frescoes of the Sistine Chapel.

From Rome, we took the train to Florence and stayed at a much nicer B&B. Florence was exquisite and Michael Angelo's David was fine. However, nothing was as wonderful as Venice. We stayed at a B&B in a family's home. They were extremely hospitable and we were somehow able to communicate without knowing Italian. Reaching the glass works in Murano in a water taxi was fun and having been a water baby I love cities, like Venice, Istanbul, and the River Walk in San Antonio, Texas.

3	large eggs
½ cup	sugar
1 cup	espresso or strong coffee
2 tblsps	Cognac or Brandy
8 ozs	Mascarpone cheese
⅛ cup	cocoa
20	ladyfingers

SERVING SIZE: 8 PREPARATION TIME: 30 MINUTES

Combine 3 egg yolks, 1 tblsp espresso, sugar and cognac in a large mixing bowl. Beat for 2 to 3 minutes. Add mascarpone cheese and beat 3 to 5 minutes until consistency is smooth.

In another bowl, combine 3 egg whites and a pinch of sugar. Beat until mixture forms stiff peaks.

Gently fold into mascarpone mixture.

Pour the rest of the espresso or other coffee into a flat dish. Dip one side of each ladyfinger in the espresso and layer them on the bottom of a serving dish. Spread ⅓ of mascarpone mixture and sprinkle cocoa. Continue layering and finish with a mascarpone layer.

Sprinkle cocoa and refrigerate.

Note: I use English Nescafe coffee for this dish.

CHEESECAKE

A cake I adapted from a recipe given to me by one of my old bosses named Ted Palowski when I was a young engineering graduate, working at our company's headquarters in Upper Saddle River, New Jersey. This is very simple to make and can be topped with fruit as well, and made as one cake or small mini cheesecakes.

CRUST

1 pkg	**Honey Maid Graham crackers, crumbled or 1 ¼ cups of graham cracker crumbs**
3 tblsps	**sugar**
3 ozs	**butter, melted**
	touch of cinnamon

SERVING SIZE: 8 PREPARATION TIME: 45 MINS

Preheat oven to 350°F

Mix crumbs, sugar and cinnamon with a fork, add melted butter and mix. Place in the bottom of a cheese cake pan where the sides unlock or a deep dish pie pan. Use a small glass upside down and press to form the pie crust.

FILLING

3 pkgs	**cream cheese (8 ozs each) at room temperature**
1 cup	**sugar**
4	**eggs**
1 tsp	**vanilla**

Beat the cream cheese and sugar together for 2 minutes.

Add eggs, one at a time, and continue beating.

Add vanilla and beat until fluffy.

Pour filling into prepared pie crust and bake at 350°F for 35 minutes.

Remove from the oven and let cool for 20 minutes.

Preheat oven to 375°F.

TOPPING

1 pint	**sour cream**
4 tblsps	**sugar,**
1 tsp	**vanilla**

Mix sour cream, sugar and vanilla together. Spread on cooled cheesecake and return to the oven and bake at 375°F degrees for 5 minutes.

Remove from the oven and let it cool. Refrigerate for several hours before serving.

Note:
For the holidays this recipe can be adapted to make 24 cupcakes:

- *Place aluminum foil bake cups in muffin pans and pour filling into each paper cup until half full.*
- *Bake for 30 minutes. Let them cool for 20 minutes and add topping and follow directions above.*

STICKY TOFFEE PUDDING

My mother made this dish famous among our circle of friends before it became popular several years ago. Some people who don't like desserts, like Nirushan, a family friend, loves this and so does my dearest cousin aunt Indu, my childhood friend. We had our own sisterhood growing up on the same street and being in the same class in school. My mother spent her school holidays with Indu's parents, her Uncle Alfred and Aunty Rajeswari, as her parents lived in Kayts and mom went to St. Bridget's convent in the city of Colombo. I try to make this dessert for Indu every time I visit Sri Lanka.

For my closest friend Ramola's 50th birthday, her family and I threw her a surprise party and I made a Mexican meal. I brought some products from Malaysia and remembered going to Colpetty wet market to try to find some Mexican products. It brought back memories of shopping at the wet market with my mother and sister when I was young. Of course, I was late getting the dessert ready as I had forgotten to make the sauce and I convinced the guests that this dish was an aphrodisiac, and they went over the moon when I served it.

This dish has become my signature dish but it is really my mother's, whose tradition I carry on, so all who knew her can continue to enjoy it.

Several restaurants all over the world serve it and some are off the mark because they make a date cake and pour butterscotch sauce over it. The cake in this dessert is made differently where it isn't as sweet as a date cake.

(CONT'D ON NEXT PAGE)

STICKY TOFFEE PUDDING (CON'TD)

THE CAKE

Prepare one 9 inch square or one 9 inch round baking pan by buttering the bottom and sides. Cut wax paper to fit the bottom of the pan (9 inch square or round). Place wax paper in the bottom of the pan and butter the top of the wax paper.

¾ cup	sugar
2 ozs	butter (½ stick)
1	egg, slightly beaten
1 cup	flour
½ tsp	baking powder
½ tsp	baking soda
½ cup	boiling water
4 ozs	dates, chopped

SERVING SIZE: 8 PREPARATION TIME: 1 HR 15 MINS

Preheat oven to 350°F.

Beat butter and sugar until creamy. Add egg and beat for 1 minute.

In a metal or ceramic bowl, combine the chopped dates and baking soda. Pour the boiling water over the date mixture.

Leave for 2 minutes.

Sift flour with baking powder. Fold ⅓ cup flour mixture into butter, sugar, egg mixture (cake batter). Add date mixture into cake batter and mix. Fold in rest of flour mixture.

Pour into the prepared cake pan and bake for 30 minutes and test by inserting a skewer into cake and if it comes out clean it is cooked . If it does not come out clean, bake it longer.

Cool cake and remove from pan and place in a glass dish that is at least 10 inch round or 10 inch square depending on the shape of the cake. Pierce holes in the cake with a skewer or fork.

THE SAUCE
1 stick butter (4 oz)
⅔ cup dark brown sugar
1 cup heavy whipping cream

Mix all ingredients together and cook on slow fire (low heat) until the mixture becomes thick and bubbly about 15 to 20 minutes.

The cake and sauce can be prepared ahead and assembled by pouring the sauce over the cake and microwaving it for 3 to 5 minutes until warm and bubbly.

Note: Both cake and sauce can be made ahead and frozen and thawed when ready to use.

To make larger cakes:
- To serve 30 people- Quadruple the recipe and use a rectangular pan 9 inches by 13 inches and an 8 inch square or round pan.
- To serve 50 people - Use 8 times the batter and an assortment of smaller baking pans or two baking pans 13 inches by 19 inches and then cut the cakes up to fit into glass dishes that can be placed in a microwave.

BUTTER CAKE

A typical Sri Lankan cake made by people from all walks of life, from village to city folk, and can be found at all the bakeries in Sri Lanka. My mother turned it into a light cake that melts in your mouth.

The other day I was making a birthday cake for my friend Sathi, and I also made some cupcakes. Unfortunately due to my oven that bakes unevenly six of my cupcakes were burnt at the bottom. It made me think of a Christmas vacation in Sri Lanka with my son and sister's family before Neesha my younger niece was born.

My cousin Suresh got a house in Nuwara Eliya where the tea plantations are and his brothers Arjuna and Indrajit joined us as well. We had a great cook at this company house but he was sometimes into his cups. One day we asked him to make us butter cake for high tea that afternoon. We went off to the Grand Hotel and, when we returned for tea, the cook came out as proud as can be staggering, of course, and served us burnt butter cake. We were looking forward to it so much that we cut off the burnt edges and ate the cake anyway.

½ lb	or 1 cup butter
½ lb	or 1 cup sugar
5	eggs
2 tsps	vanilla
½ lb	or 2 cups flour less ⅛ cup (less ¼ cup for chocolate cake)
2 tsps	baking powder
¼ cup	milk
¼ cup	cocoa powder, optional for chocolate cake

SERVING SIZE: 8 PREPARATION TIME: 1:00

Preheat oven to 375°F.

Prepare two 8 inch square or two 8 inch round baking pans by buttering the bottom and sides. Cut wax paper to fit the bottom of the pan (8 inch square or round). Place wax paper in the bottom of the pan and butter the top of the wax paper.

Sift flour and baking powder and leave aside. (For chocolate cake add cocoa to flour and sift).

Place butter and sugar in a mixing bowl and beat with an electric mixer until creamy, about 5 minutes. Add eggs to butter cream mixture, one at a time. Continue beating. Add vanilla and continue beating. Fold in flour alternately with milk.

Bake for 20 minutes in the center of the oven. Insert a wooden skewer and if it comes out clean take the cake out of the oven.

If it does not come out clean, bake it longer.

Let cool for 10 minutes or so and remove from pan using a knife to loosen the sides and place on a wire rack to cool further. Remove wax paper from the cakes.

Note: to make larger cakes:

- To make two 9 inch by 13 inch rectangular cakes, triple the quantity of batter.
- For two sheet cakes use four times the quantity of batter shown above.
- This recipe can also be used to make 24 cup cakes. Place bake cups in muffin pans and pour cake batter into each paper cup until half full. Bake for 20 minutes or until a wooden skewer comes out clean. Let them cool and remove from pan.

BUTTER CREAM FROSTING

½ lb **butter**
1 lb **confectioners sugar (icing) sugar, sifted**
½ tsp **vanilla**
¼ cup **milk, (add more milk for chocolate frosting)**
2 tblsps **cocoa, sifted, optional for chocolate frosting**

Place butter and icing sugar (and cocoa for chocolate frosting) in a mixing bowl and beat with an electric mixer until creamy, about 5 minutes. Add vanilla and milk. Beat until fluffy.

Place one of the cakes on a cake plate. Spread frosting on top and place the other cake on top of the frosted cake. Spread a very thin layer of frosting on the top and sides of the assembled cake and leave aside for about 15 minutes. This is called crumb coating and it seals the cake.

Use remaining frosting to complete the icing of the cake. The cup cakes are easier to frost. Use a knife to spread the icing on top of the cupcakes or use an icing bag with a flower nozzle to make it decorative.

Note: Use Dutch cocoa for chocolate cake and chocolate frosting.

CHOCOLATE CHIP CAKE

A yummy cake loved by children. I got the recipe from a co-worker from years past called Marvin, in Wellesley, Massachusetts. It is very tasty and the fastest cake I make and it is great with a steaming cup of coffee and ideal for high tea. Growing up in Sri Lanka, high tea was a daily event after school. On weekdays it was a savory and a sweet dish. On weekends, it was Chocolate cake from Green Cabin, patties, sandwiches, cutlets and little Sri Lankan cheesecakes. When we had high tea at my aunt Girlie's house it included a heavenly Battenberg cake made by her. Her daughter, my cousin Lakshmi, is also an excellent cook and always hosts a high tea for me when I visit Sri Lanka.

1 stick	(4 ozs) butter	1 tsp	baking powder
1 pkg	(8 oz) cream cheese	¼ tsp	salt
1 cup	sugar	¼ tsp	baking soda
2	eggs	½ cup	milk
1 tsp	vanilla	1 lg pkg	chocolate chips (12 ozs)
2 cups	flour		

SERVING SIZE: 8 PREPARATION TIME: 1 HR 30 MIN

Preheat oven to 350°F.

Prepare a Bundt baking pan by buttering the bottom and sides.

Sift flour, baking powder, baking soda and salt and leave aside.

Place butter, sugar and cream cheese in a mixing bowl and beat with an electric mixer until creamy, about 5 minutes.

Add eggs to butter and cream cheese mixture, one at a time. Continue beating. Add vanilla and beat for 2 minutes.

Mix in flour, baking powder and soda by hand using a spatula. Add milk and chocolate chips and continue to mix by hand.

Pour batter into prepared Bundt pan and bake at 350°F for about 1 hour.

Watch the cake by looking at it after 45 minutes of baking time and by inserting a wooden skewer and if it comes out clean, take the cake out of the oven. If it does not come out clean, bake it longer.

Let cool and invert onto a cake tray, slice and serve.

RIBBON CAKE

A divine Ribbon cake made by my dearest friend Suki Wanigatunge's mother, Therese Moonesinghe, who was an exceptional cook and immigrated to Los Angeles with her husband and children a couple of years after we moved to Boston. A few years later I was honored to be a bridesmaid at Suki and Rohan's wedding.

This cake is multi colored where one layer is pink and the other is green. The Hilton Hotel in Colombo makes a California ribbon cake with a brownie in the middle. It is delicious. My ribbon cake makes everyone think it has a touch of coconut flavor. But the truth is, I add vanilla in its purest form which I get from Mexico or Salvador and it seems to have a taste which hints at coconut.

8	eggs
1 lb	or 3 ¾ cups flour
1 lb	or 2 cups sugar
1 lb	or 4 sticks butter
3 tsps	baking powder
1 tsp	vanilla

SERVING SIZE: 16 PEOPLE PREPARATION TIME: 2 HRS

Prepare two 10 inch round baking pans by buttering the bottom and sides. Cut wax paper to fit the bottom of the pans. Place wax paper in the bottom of the pans and butter the top of the wax paper.

Preheat oven to 300°F

Cream the butter and sugar until creamy. Add eggs, one at a time, and continue beating. Add vanilla. Sift flour and baking powder, and fold into butter and sugar mixture.

Separate the batter into two bowls of equal proportions. Add a dash of food coloring, pink into one bowl and green in the other bowl and mix. Pour the green batter into one baking pan and the pink batter into the other.

Bake for 30 minutes or until a wooden skewer comes out clean. Let cool and remove from pan.

Note (to make larger cakes):
- *For 50 people: Make a batch which is 1 ½ times the recipe, split the batter and use two 9 x 13 inch rectangular pans.*
- *For 100 people: Use two 13 x 19 inch baking pans and two batches of the batter (one batch is 1 ½ times the recipe) which is a total of three times the recipe.*

FROST WITH BUTTERCREAM ICING (Page 99)

For the rectangular cake that serves 50 people use 1 ½ times the icing recipe. For the much larger cake that serves 100 people use 3 times the recipe to sandwich and frost the cake.

OR, the traditional method of icing of the cake is:

- Sandwich the two cakes with the buttercream frosting.
- Boil apricot jam with a little water for a few minutes. This is called the apricot wash.
- Put a sheet of marzipan on top of the cake after brushing cake with the apricot wash.
- Brush the marzipan with the apricot wash and put the royal icing on top of the cake.
- Put royal icing on the sides of the cake.

The groom having a smoke with his army buddies, Jeff Felix, Harry Gunasekara and others.

SACHER TORTE

An exquisite Sacher torte demonstrated to all of us at home by my mother's German friend, Elsie, who stayed with us in Boston, frequently, and taught us how to make this cake. Elsie worked with my mother and was befriended by her, as she had recently moved from Germany.

Germany has some wonderful memories for me. Gail and I had euro passes and travelled through Europe starting with Amsterdam and then headed towards Germany but, unfortunately, as it was May Day the next day we were unable to cash money so we went to a bar and partied until it was time to get on the train to Zurich. We were on our way to visit my dad's younger brother, Uncle Lakshman, and family in Geneva.

I visited Cologne, Germany, several times on business and discovered the house where 4711 the Eau De Cologne was manufactured and sold. During World War II the Nazi's identified houses by numbers instead of streets, hence 4711 got its name. In our homes in Sri Lanka, this cologne was used as a scent as well as for medicinal purposes like a headache or a fever. Our mother would immerse a face towel in cold water mixed with 4711 and put it on our foreheads to soothe the pain.

I made it to Munich as well for an aeronautical conference and enjoyed the Bavarian food. Their unique meatloaf sandwich and the famous white sausages with mustard for breakfast were my favorite. The Beer Gardens, bicycle friendly towns and other attractions which shall remain nameless was very entertaining.

CAKE

5 ozs	semisweet chocolate
¾ cup	sugar
¾ cup	butter
5	eggs, separated
¾ cup	flour, sifted
2 tblsp	rum, optional
½	bottle apricot jam

SERVING SIZE: 8 PREPARATION TIME: 2 HOURS

Preheat oven to 325°F.

Melt semi-sweet chocolate in a double boiler and let cool.

Place butter and sugar in a mixing bowl and beat in an electric mixer until fluffy.

Beat in gradually egg yolks until mixture turns light colored. Add cooled melted chocolate and mix.

Add flour and the rum and mix. Beat egg whites until it becomes stiff, but NOT DRY.

Fold beaten egg whites into the cake batter.

Bake in an ungreased 8 or 9 inch round pan for 50 to 60 minutes or until a wooden skewer comes out clean.

Let cool and remove from pan.

EUROPEAN ICING

4 ozs	chocolate
2 tblsp	heavy or whipping cream
2 tblsp	rum
1 ⅓ cup	icing (confectioners) sugar

Melt chocolate in a double boiler. Add cream, rum and icing sugar and mix.

Slice the cake horizontally in half and spread it with apricot jam. Frost the top and sides of the cake with European icing.

COOKING FOR CHILDREN

As shown through a mother's love.

My earliest memories include riding as a little girl on the back of my uncle Bole's motorcycle, as well as on the back of my father's Army horse "Pink Lane". I often wonder about my love for horses and attraction to men who ride motorcycles!

CHICKEN ENCHILADAS

I always make this when I do a Mexican Buffet as it is a subtle and appetizing dish. The recipe was given to me by Gail, my friend of forty three years, who picked it up from some old lady cooking Mexican food while she was visiting Colorado somewhere near Denver.

I spent many a vacation in different parts of Mexico, when my son was a baby. One year it was Puerto Vallarta, another was Acapulco, then Cozumel and, finally, Cancun. I found the food in Mexico to be delicious, especially the carne asada, a grilled meat dish.

This story reminds me of my experience in another Spanish speaking country in South America. I was in Peru for work and went to Machu Picchu for the weekend with my colleague and friend Deone, and the local director arranged for us to have a guide to tour the area and, when we stopped for lunch, he ordered the local delicacy and out of courtesy I had to eat Guinea pig, which came to the table all stuffed with crushed basil leaves. Deone is a Pescatarian, and gracefully declined.

That year my friend Phuong gave me a small guinea pig stuffed animal for a Christmas present.

2	**whole chickens**
1 cup	**sour cream**
1 cup	**Longhorn (or cheddar) cheese, shredded**
1 tsp	**salt**
½ tsp	**pepper**
½ tsp	**ground cumin**
1 pkg	**(10 each) 8 inch round flour tortillas**

SERVING SIZE: 5 PREPARATION TIME: 2 HRS

Boil chickens in a large pot of water. Remove skin and shred them (take chicken off the bone). Add sour cream and shredded cheese and mix into the chicken. Add salt, pepper and ground cumin and mix.

Preheat oven to 350°F

Heat a frying pan on high heat and put in the tortilla, and once heated, turn it over. When both sides are heated, place the tortilla on a plate lined with paper towels. Place a paper towel in between each tortilla as well.

Put a heaping amount of filling in each tortilla, roll them, and put them in a baking pan. Add grated cheese on top.

Bake until cheese melts. Approximately 15 minutes.

SAUCE

½ lb	good pork shoulder, cut up into small cubes.
2 cans	diced tomatoes and green chilies (10 oz cans)
½ cup	flour
½ cup	oil
¼ tsp	salt
¼ tsp	pepper
¼ tsp	ground cumin

Shake the pork cubes in a small bag with flour and fry on high heat in a small frying pan with some oil until brown. Add the 2 cans of tomatoes and green chili and mix. Add salt, pepper and cumin and let the sauce simmer for about 5 minutes.

Place the enchiladas on a serving platter and pour the sauce over it and serve.

Note: The sauce can be made without the pork cubes by mixing the cans of tomatoes and green chili with the salt, pepper and cumin and simmer for 5 minutes.

CHICKEN TENDERS PEPE STYLE

A delish dish I created while my son was a young boy and, about a year ago, I asked my friend Sammy Gail about her original fried chicken recipe and she gave me a few hints that I incorporated into this recipe. My niece, Shivani, grew up eating chicken as her mother was a "chicketarian" when she was born, and my son Michael Selvan loves chicken tenders, so to entice the kids to eat homemade food, I worked on this recipe.

Have you ever had chicken and waffles? It is Southern fried chicken served with waffles and maple syrup as a main entrée at Southern restaurants in the USA. I particularly love the chicken and waffles at Marvin, a restaurant in Washington DC, named after Marvin Gaye.

1 lb	**boneless chicken breast**
1 cup	**flour**
½ cup	**milk**
1	**egg beaten**
Salt and pepper to taste	

SERVING SIZE: 4 PREPARATION TIME: 1 HR

Slice chicken horizontally in half and then cut into 1 to 1 ½ inch wide strips. Dip in milk and then dip in flour mixed with salt and pepper. Dip in egg and then dip again in seasoned flour.

Heat oil at medium high temperature, in a deep flat frying pan or deep fryer until hot. Fry chicken until golden brown. Remove from fire and place on paper towels to drain the oil.

Arrange on a platter and serve with homemade French fries (peel and cut baking potatoes into thin or thick strips and deep fry).

Note: Fry potatoes in oil first and then fry chicken in the same oil together with an additional inch of new oil.

FIVE FLAVORED CHICKEN

I ate this dish at a Chinese restaurant when I was living in New Brunswick, New Jersey, more than thirty years ago and the owners shared this recipe in the newspaper write up about the restaurant. I have treasured this recipe since then, and shared it with my mother and sister. I have also changed it, slightly. The key to the success of this recipe is not to overcook the chicken when you are frying it at the beginning since it is returned to the wok to add the sauce.

My son loves this dish and, as difficult as he was about food, this dish he ate. That's how it found its way into this section of the book.

3 cups	**vegetable oil**
1 lb	**boneless skinless chicken breasts**
1 cup	**steamed broccoli florets**

Cut chicken into 1 to 1 ½ inch square and ¼ inch thick pieces and place in a plastic container with a lid.

MARINADE
1 egg
¼ tsp garlic powder
1 tblsp cornstarch
1 tblsp sweet sherry
1 tblsp water
Dash of salt and pepper
Mix the above ingredients and add to the chicken, and mix. Marinade the chicken for at least 2 hours in the refrigerator.

SAUCE
1 ½ tblsps sherry
1 ½ tblsps vinegar
3 tblsps soy sauce
3 tblsps sugar
Mix sauce ingredients together in a small bowl.
½ tsp cornstarch
½ tblsp water

SERVING SIZE: 4 PREPARATION TIME: 1 HR 30 MIN

When ready to cook, heat the oil in a wok until medium hot and fry chicken until ready, but not quite done. Remove chicken and all but 2 tblsps of oil. Drain chicken on paper towels.

Put the chicken back in the wok and add the sauce, mix and fry for a few seconds. Mix cornstarch with water and add to chicken to thicken. When chicken looks glazed and thick about 2 minutes, take off the fire.

Put chicken in the centre of a dish and place steamed broccoli florets around it and serve with white rice preferably Jasmine.

Note: Served as an entree with other dishes makes 8 servings.

STICKY CHICKEN

My Japanese American carpool buddy, Rod Sato, told me how to make this chicken dish while driving to work one morning from Toms River, New Jersey, to Atlantic City. Since then it has become a popular dish in my house.

I was very ignorant about some of the history of Japanese Americans during World War II and he enlightened me on the subject. There are so many people I met years ago that I have lost touch with but remember them fondly.

1 lb	**boneless skinless chicken breast**
1 cup	**breadcrumbs**
1	**egg, beaten**
1 cup	**oil**
¼ cup	**soy sauce**
¼ cup	**honey**
Salt and pepper	

SERVING SIZE: 4 PREPARATION TIME: 45 MINUTES

Cut chicken into 1 inch square and ½ inch thick pieces.

Add salt and pepper to egg. Dip chicken pieces in egg and dip in breadcrumbs.

Heat oil at medium high temperature, in a deep flat frying pan or deep fryer until hot.

Fry chicken until golden brown (do not overcook as the chicken will be hard when mixed with the sauce).

Remove from fire and place on paper towels to drain the oil.

Mix soy sauce and honey in a medium saucepan and heat on a medium high fire until boiling. Let simmer for 2 minutes.

Add chicken and mix so the sauce coats the chicken and heat for a few minutes until chicken is hot.

Serve with white rice, preferably Jasmine.

SHEPHERD'S PIE

I grew up eating the Ceylonese version of this dish and it was only after I met my dear friend, Lyn, in Malaysia did I taste the original English pie and it was scrumptious. We met as our children were classmates at the international school in Kuantan. Unlike the other expatriate women who lived in Kuantan, I was a working mother in a satellite ground earth station, with all local men and two Malay women.

I never met any of the international crowd until Lyn invited us to a barbecue on the beach in Cherating, about 30 minutes from Kuantan. Everybody brought a dish; we barbecued, ate, and the children gathered the wood.

SHEPHERD'S PIE (CON'TD)

for a bonfire, which we lit after dinner and someone, invariably, told ghost stories. The bonfire was heavenly and something I really miss, living on the East Coast of the USA. They seem to be able to light them in California.

The barbecues became a weekly ritual with us as we had to make our own fun since we lived in a remote area of Malaysia, Both, the adults and the children, had a lot of fun.

1 lb	ground beef		1 cube	beef stock
2 tblsps	tomato puree or tomato paste		¾ liter	boiling water
2 tblsps	ketchup		1 med	onion, chopped
½ tsp	salt		2 tblsps	oil
⅛ tsp	pepper		2 large	baking potatoes
2 tblsps	Bisto gravy thickener and 1 tsp cornstarch (or 2 tblsp cornstarch)		3 tblsps	butter
			⅔ cup	grated cheddar cheese
½ cup	cold water		2 cups	cooked vegetables, optional
1 tsp	Worcestershire sauce			

SERVING SIZE: 4 PREPARATION TIME: 1 HR 30 MINS

Preheat oven to 350°F

Heat oil at medium high temperature, in a deep flat frying pan. Fry onion until glazed. Add beef, salt and pepper, tomato puree and ketchup. Melt stock cube in ¾ liter of boiling water. Pour ⅓ stock into meat and let it simmer for 5 minutes.

Mix 1 tblsp Bisto gravy powder with the cold water and 1 tsp cornstarch or 2 tblsp cornstarch mixed with cold water.

Add Worcestershire sauce and mix. Pour half of the mixture into meat and keep stirring until thickened. Put meat in a glass dish and spread evenly.

Pour the remaining stock into the pan the meat was in, add the remaining Bisto gravy or cornstarch into the pan and cook until thickened and leave aside.

In the meantime, boil potatoes and drain. Add salt and pepper to taste and butter, and beat with a fork. Lay potatoes over the meat and spread evenly. Sprinkle grated cheddar on top and bake until brown, about 20 to 30 minutes

The remaining gravy is poured on the cooked vegetables and served with the Shepherd's pie.

Note: Bisto gravy thickener is available in England. I use the cornstarch only.

VASANTHICA'S SPECIAL DRINK

Watermelons bring back my college years in Boston, going to outdoor concerts, and the sun beating down on us, naked hippies all over the place, from children to adults, and people eating slices of watermelon, trying to stay cool.

This was my mother's special creation and a perfect ending to the cookbook and her culinary journey through life using her exceptional talent to create and dazzle her guests with her delicious dishes that ranged from appetizers to dessert.

¼	of a medium size watermelon
½ cup	sugar syrup (lessen or increase to taste)
⅓ cup	lime juice (lessen or increase to taste)
½ liter	ginger ale or 7-up

SERVING SIZE: 6 PREPARATION TIME: 20 MINUTES

Cut up skinned watermelon. Put it in a blender (without seeds). Crush and strain it through a strainer twice.

Add sugar syrup and lime juice to taste. Refrigerate and when ready to serve mix with Ginger Ale or Seven-Up.

Note: To make sugar syrup, put sugar and some water in a bowl and microwave for a few minutes until the sugar is dissolved

The bride dressed in her "Koorai" sari as they depart the reception.

GLOSSARY

APRICOT JAM: Made with apricots, a small fruit with a thin, velvety, orange skin and a meaty golden cream flesh inside.

APRICOT NECTAR: The sweet liquid of an apricot fruit.

ASIAN PUMPKIN: A vegetable which is a gourd-like squash. There are many varieties of pumpkins and the North American variety is bright orange in color but the Asian pumpkin is light orange with flecks of green. Do not substitute Halloween pumpkins for Asian pumpkins in the recipes.

BAKING POWDER: A derivative of baking soda. Baking powder is a double action leavener that is activated when mixed with a liquid.

BAMBOO SKEWERS: A thin wooden stick used to skewer meats, vegetables and fruits.

BEEF STOCK: A thin soup, or a liquid such as water in which beef has been cooked.

BLACK MUSTARD SEEDS: The black variety of mustard seed, which is smaller and more pungent than the yellow variety. In Sri Lankan cooking we do not substitute with a lighter seed.

BLACK PEPPER GROUND OR SEEDS: A flowering vine whose fruit is usually dried and used as a spice and seasoning. Cooked and dried unripe fruit is black pepper, green pepper is the dried unripe fruit and white pepper is the dried ripe seed.

BRANDY: A spirit produced by distilling wine and taken as an after-dinner drink and used in cooking in many parts of the world.

BRAZIL NUTS: A South American tree with a large odd shaped nut and a great substitute for Kemeri or Candle nuts which are only available in Asian markets.

BREAD CRUMBS: Made from days old bread, cut up and baked in an oven and ground into crumbs.

BROCCOLI FLORETS: Italian for cabbage sprout, a member of the cabbage family with emerald green florets on top of a stalk with dark green leaves.

BROWN SUGAR: A white sugar mixed with molasses. To create, add two tablespoons molasses to one cup white sugar.

CAPSICUMS: A large variety of chili with a long pod large enough to stuff with spiced meat or fish mixtures.

CARROTS: A root vegetable, orange in color.

CASHEWS: A sweet, kidney-shaped nut. Predominant in Sri Lankan cuisine as the trees grow in abundance there and in many parts of Asia and used in both sweet and savory cooking. Available as raw cashews in Asian markets and as distinct from the roasted and salted cashews sold as snacks.

CASTER SUGAR: British term for superfine granulated sugar.

CAYENNE PEPPER: A red, hot chili pepper used to flavor dishes and named after the city of Cayenne in French Guiana.

CELERY SEEDS: Small and brown seeds from Celery, a vegetable with long stalks and commonly used in pickling, stuffing and salads.

CHICK PEAS: A type of pea native to the Mediterranean region also known as garbanzo bean and used in Indian, Sri Lankan, Middle Eastern and South American cuisine. In Sri Lanka we make a light soft snack with it called "Kadalai" with fresh coconut and dried red chilies.

CHICKEN BOUILLON: A cube of dehydrated stock that is mixed in boiling water and used in Asian cooking, soups and sauces.

CHICKEN SEASONING: A blend of ingredients used for fried chicken seasoning.

CHICKEN STOCK: A base for various dishes in many parts of Asia and prepared by boiling chicken bones and straining them.

CHILI POWDER: The dried, ground red chili of one or more varieties of chili pepper. It is used in many different cuisines, including Sri Lankan, Tex-Mex, Indian, Chinese, and Thai.

CHILI SAUCE: There are two different types of chilli sauce. The Chinese style is made from chilies, salt and vinegar, and has a hot flavor. The Malaysian, Singaporean or Sri Lankan chilli sauce is a mixture of hot, sweet and salty flavors enhanced with ginger and garlic and cooked with vinegar. Both types are available in Asian food stores.

CINNAMON STICK: True cinnamon is native to Sri Lanka. For Asian cuisine, buy cinnamon sticks rather than the ground spice, which loses its flavor when stored too long. It is used in both sweet and savory dishes.

CLOVES: Aromatic dried flower buds from a tree native to the Maluku Islands and used as a spice in cuisines all over the world.

COCOA: A brown, unsweetened powder produced by crushing cocoa nibs; and used as a flavoring; also known as unsweetened cocoa.

COCONUT MILK: An ingredient in most Southeast Asian cooking and it is not the liquid inside a coconut. It is prepared by soaking the grated flesh of a coconut in hot water (dairy free) or scalded milk, then straining the combination. Coconut milk is classified as thick, thin, or coconut cream.

COCONUT POWDER: Manufactured through a drying process and very different from the coarser desiccated coconut and made from the white coconut meat. A good substitute for fresh coconut milk when mixed with scalded milk.

COGNAC: A variety of brandy named after the town of Cognac in France, and produced in the same region.

CONFECTIONERS SUGAR: A refined sugar ground into a fine powder; also known as powdered sugar and 10X sugar.

CORIANDER SEEDS: The seeds of the cilantro (coriander)plant; used as a spice and available whole or ground and used in Middle Eastern, Indian and Asian cuisines. It is also the primary ingredient of Sri Lankan curry powder.

CORN FLOUR AND CORN STARCH: Used as a thickening agent in soups, sauces, gravy and custards.

CRABMEAT: The meat from the crab is removed from the shells and packaged and sold in 6, 8 or 16 ounce containers. Lump crabmeat is meat from the body of the crab and does not include the claws.

CRAB SHELLS: The top shell of the crab which comes off easily from the body and the legs.

CREAM CHEESE: A soft, mild cheese made from cow's cream and used for baking, dips, dressings, confections and spreading on bagels;

CUMIN SEEDS: Together with coriander, the most essential ingredient in curry powders and the only two in my mother's curry powder. It is available as seed, or ground.

CURRY LEAVES: Available in Asian food markets, fresh but can be purchased dried as well. The tree is native to Asia; the leaves are small and very shiny and can be easily grown in any sun room. Curry powder is NOT made with curry leaves.

CURRY POWDER: A mixture of spices roasted or unroasted and ground together into a powder. My mother's curry powder is a combination of Coriander and Cumin seeds. Sri Lankans use curry leaves and other spices. Indians use turmeric in the curry powder. Each country makes their unique curry powder with their own combination of spices.

DATES: The fruit of a palm tree native to the Middle East and Mediterranean region; eaten fresh or dried. In Sri Lanka we stuff them with marzipan and serve as a sweet or make into chutney.

DRIED SHRIMP FLAKES: Made by grinding Chinese dried shrimp available at Asian food stores with a mortar & pestle or a food processor.

DUCK SAUCE: A sweet sauce made by the Chinese for dipping wontons and egg rolls and available in bottles in supermarkets.

EGGPLANT: A vegetable that is mild in taste, and great grilled, broiled, sautéed, or roasted. Keep refrigerated.

ENGLISH MUFFINS: Little round porous flat breads sold in packages of 6 in the USA. Crumpets can be substituted in the UK and any 3 inch round flat bread can be substituted in other countries.

ESPRESSO COFFEE: A small amount of mostly Italian coffee brewed by forcing a small amount of water through finely ground coffee beans.

EVAPORATED MILK: A dehydrated canned milk product.

FENNEL POWDER: Available in ground or seed form and sometimes known as 'sweet or 'large cumin', and of the same botanical family. Seeds are used in Sri Lankan curries as a seasoning and the powder to thicken the curry.

FENUGREEK: Seed of an Asiatic herb with a bitter flavor and commonly used in seafood curries and coconut gravy.

GARLIC: A species in the onion family and used all over the world in Asian, Mediterranean, Western and European cuisines as well as South American and Caribbean cuisines.

GELATIN: A thickening agent that is dissolved in hot water and thickens whatever food it's been added to.

GINGER OR GINGER ROOT: The English name ginger comes from French however the origin is from Tamil my native language.

GRAHAM CRACKERS: Made with Graham flour and invented by Reverend Graham of Bound Brook, NJ.

GREEN CHILI: Cayenne pepper before it turns red in the sun and used like fresh red chilies.

GREEN OR RED PEPPER: Commonly called Bell peppers and hail from a domesticated species of chili pepper.

CREAM: Made from milk with a milk fat content of at least 18% and is thick and tastes richer than milk and rises to the top of raw milk when cooked. Heavy cream is used for whipping and light cream for sauces.

HONEY: A sweet thick liquid made by bees from flower nectar and stored in the cells of the hive for food. It is usually used as a natural alternative to sugar.

ITALIAN DRESSING: A salad dressing made with oil & vinegar and Italian herbs.

KECAP MANIS: Indonesian sweet soy sauce that comes in medium and sweet which is a dark soy sauce with brown sugar added to it.

KEMIRI: Known as Candlenut is from a flowering tree and used in Malaysian and Indonesian cuisine .Referred to as Indian walnut, and in Malay, Buah keras and Kemir, in Indonesian.

LADYFINGER COOKIES: a small finger-shaped sponge cake that looks like a cookie.

LAOS POWDER: A very delicate spice, sold in powder form, laos comes from the dried root of the' greater galangal'. It is so delicate in flavor that it can be omitted from recipes.

LEMON: A citrus fruit with a bright yellow skin, and oval in shape, juicy yellow flesh and a very tart flavor and similar to limes and easily substituted.

LEMON GRASS: A tall grass with sharp-edged leaves that adds a lemony flavor to curries. Cut one stem with a knife, close to the root, and use 4- 5 inches of the stalk. 12 strips dried lemon grass are equal to one fresh stem or 2 strips of thinly peeled lemon rind can be substituted.

LIME: Easy substitute for lemons and the juice of this fruit is used in Sri Lanka and other Asian countries for adding a sour flavor to curries and other dishes. Lemons are sometimes hard to find in Asia and limes can be used instead.

LINGUINE: Long, narrow, slightly flattened strands of pasta.

MALDIVES FISH: Dried tuna from the Maldives Islands, used extensively in Sri Lankan cooking and sold in packets, broken into small chips. Substitute dried prawn powder.

MANGO PUREE: Crushed and blended form of the tropical fruit called mango which is yellow, shaded red when ripe, and is peeled before eating.

MARGARINE: A substitute for butter and made from animal or vegetable fat and butter flavored.

MARIE BISCUITS: A sweet biscuit made with wheat flour, sugar, vegetable oil and vanilla. The biscuit is round and very popular in Western, Middle Eastern and Asian countries and is also available with Spanish and Latino Products and called "Maria" biscuits.

MASCARPONE CHEESE: Considered a cheese, but it is actually pasteurized cream that tastes fresh and spreadable and used in Italian desserts, like Tiramisu, and a great topping for green salads and fruit salads.

MAYONNAISE: Cold, thick, creamy sauce made of oil and vinegar emulsified with egg yolks and used as a spread for sandwiches, a salad dressing or dip.

MINT SAUCE: There are many varieties, but the common, round-leafed mint is the one most often used in cooking.1t adds flavor to many curries, salads, drinks and Middle Eastern dishes.

MUSHROOM: The popular species consists of a stem, a cap and considered a vegetable; available fresh or dried and in many different varieties, sizes and colors and enjoyed in almost all cuisines around the world.

NUTMEG: Hard seed of a yellow fruit from a native Asian tree and has an oval shape and smooth texture with a strong, sweet aroma and flavor; used ground or grated in sweet and savory dishes.

OLD ENGLISH CHEESE SPREAD: In the US this cheese spread is sold in a small jar with a blue top and called Old English Cheese spread. A sharp cheddar cheese spread can be substituted for this.

OLIVE OIL: All-purpose oil that comes in two different varieties: "extra-virgin" olive oil from the first cold pressing of olives; and "pure" olive oil, which is a lower grade but the extra light is great for healthier cooking as it is a pure vegetable oil. I use it in my curries.

ONION: Available in many varieties, sweet such as Vidalia in the USA and Red Bermuda onion which is a mild onion for raw salads. Shallots in the West are called Red onions, in Sri Lanka and the larger onions are called Bombay onions in Sri Lanka and red onions in other parts of Asia.

OREGANO: A member of the mint family, used in Italian and Greek cuisine.

PAPRIKA: Spice made from ground, dried Capsicum either bell pepper or chili pepper varieties. The seasoning is used in many cuisines to add color and flavor to dishes. Paprika can range from mild to hot. It is a good substitute for chili powder for those who can't eat hot, spicy foods.

PARMESAN CHEESE: A hard, granular cheese made from raw cow's milk that is cooked but not pressed. It is named after the producing areas in Italy but the name is derived from the French word for hard cheese.

PARSLEY: Herb with several varieties such as fresh Italian flat leaf or curly parsley used in salad recipes. Chopped, it can be used in salads or baked dishes.

PEANUT: A legume and not a nut and used for snacking, baking, for making peanut butter and chopped, it is used as a garnish in Asian cuisine.

PEANUT BUTTER: A buttery paste primarily composed of roasted peanuts and loved by kids all over the world.

PEANUT OIL: Also known as groundnut oil is a mild vegetable oil made from peanuts.

PEPPER: Black pepper, a fruit which is usually dried and used as a spice and seasoning.

PINE NUTS: A tangy flavored nut reminiscent of pine, used in Mediterranean dishes.

PINEAPPLE: A fruit native to Sri Lanka with a diamond-patterned, spiny, and greenish-brown skin ; juicy yellow flesh with a hard core center and a sweet-sour flavor.

PITA BREAD: Unleavened bread in Mediterranean and Middle Eastern cuisine..

PORK: The culinary name used for domestic pig, which is eaten in many countries.

PRESTO GRAVY: A gravy mix available in England and used in Shepherd's pie.

RAISINS: A sweet dried grape.

RED (BERMUDA) ONION: Red in color and not irritating to the throat when eaten raw. In Asia they are small in size and the most commonly used onion.

RED CHILIES: A vey spicy fresh red pepper used in Sri Lankan and Asian cuisine.

RED PEPPER FLAKES: Crushed red pepper, made from a mix of different varieties of hot dried red peppers.

RICE: A gluten-free starch seed in three sizes or types; long-grain, medium-grain and short-grain, and available in different processed forms; white, brown rice and parboiled rice which is Basmati.

SALT: One of the oldest forms of food seasoning, and an important method of food preservation. Saltiness is one of the basic human tastes.

SAMBAL OLEK: Raw chili paste bright red and very spicy originating in Indonesia. Oelek is the Dutch spelling for the special stoneware from the village of Basalt.

SCALLIONS: Green onions, spring onions, all of which look like onions with hollow green leaves and a small root bulb.

SESAME OIL: Extracted from toasted sesame seed and used in Chinese cooking.

SESAME SEEDS: Black sesame and white sesame seeds are used in Korean, Chinese and Japanese food, as well as in desserts in the Middle East and in Southeast Asian countries.

SHRIMP: Crustaceans' found widely around the world in both fresh and salt water. Warm water and cold water shrimp vary both in size and taste from jumbo to small shrimp,.

SOUR CREAM: A dairy product made by fermenting a regular cream with certain kinds of lactic acid bacteria.

SOY SAUCE: Predominantly used in Chinese cooking and comes in two varieties light and dark soy sauce. Indonesians use a dark sweet soy sauce called "kecap manis" which has brown sugar added to it.

SUGAR: Common name for a class of sweet-flavored substances used in food. It has been produced in the Indian subcontinent since ancient times and available in white and brown sugars, natural and processed.

SUGAR SYRUP: Sugar dissolved in water.

SULTANAS: Golden raisins.

SWEET BANANA PEPPERS: Yellow wax pepper or banana chili or sweet, is a medium-sized member of the chili pepper family that has a mild, tangy taste.

SWEET RELISH: A chopped pickled cucumber condiment eaten with hot dogs or hamburgers.

SWEET SHERRY: A Sweet dessert wine.

SWEETENED COCONUT FLAKES: Usually made by Angel foods in the USA, but slightly sweetened fresh grated coconut can be substituted.

TAHINI: A paste made from crushed sesame seeds and used to flavor Middle Eastern dishes. When combined with a little oil, it is used as a spread on bread. Peanut butter can be substituted.

TAMARIND: Sour tasting fruit of a large tropical tree that is dried, and sold in packets. Used in Sri Lankan curries as tamarind liquid. Soak a piece of tamarind the size of a walnut in half a cup of hot water for10 minutes until soft, then squeezing it until it mixes with the water and strain.

TOMATO: Botanically a fruit and considered a vegetable for culinary purposes. Common to all cuisines of the world and is available in various varieties Beefsteak, Plum, Cherry etc... Eaten raw and as an ingredient in many dishes, sauces, and in drinks.

TURMERIC: From the ginger family, turmeric with its orange-yellow color is a mainstay of curries. It should never be confused with true saffron and the two may not be used interchangeably.

VANILLA: Vanilla comes in two forms as beans and extract. These recipes use vanilla extract. When using pure vanilla from Mexico or South and Central America, use half the quantity in the recipe.

VEGETABLE OIL: A blended oil of different vegetable oils such as corn, safflower, rapeseed, cottonseed and soybean oils.

VINEGAR: A liquid combination of acetic acid and water.

WATER CHESTNUTS: A Chinese aquatic vegetable which is not a nut. Available in tinned slices or whole and is a popular ingredient in Chinese dishes.

WATERMELON: The fruit of an annual plant that has a green skin and bright pink flesh eaten by various cultures all over the world.

WHITE VINEGAR: Distilled vinegar.

WINE VINEGAR: Made from red or white wine.

WONTON SKINS: Small squares of fresh noodle dough available at Chinese grocery stores in the refrigerator section.

WORCESTERSHIRE SAUCE: A fermented liquid condiment used in Western cuisine.

YOGURT: A milk food produced by bacterial fermentation of milk. The recipes in this book calls for unflavored yogurt.

CONVERSION CHARTS

OVEN TEMPERATURES

Mark	Degrees Farenheit	Degrees Celsius
1	275	140
2	300	150
3	325	170
4	350	180
5	375	190
6	400	200
7	425	220
8	450	230
9	475	240

VOLUME

British	Metric
2 fl oz	55 ml
3 fl oz	75 ml
5 (¼ pt)	150 ml
½ pt	275 ml
¾ pt	425 ml
1 pt	570 ml
1 ¼ pt	725 ml
1 ¾ pt	1 L
2 pt	1.2 L
2 ½ pt	1.5 L
4 pt	2.25 L

WEIGHTS

British	Metric	British	Metric
½ oz	10 g	6 oz	175 g
¾ oz	20 g	7 oz	200 g
1 oz	25 g	8 oz	225 g
1 ½ oz	40 g	9 oz	250 g
2 oz	50 g	10 oz	275 g
2 ½ oz	60 g	12 oz	350 g
3 oz	75 g	1 lb	450 g
4 oz	110 g	1 ½ lb	700 g
4 ½ oz	125 g	2 lb	900 g
5 oz	150 g	3 lb	1.35 Kg